5.95

Longman
Simplified English Series

JAMAICA INN

LONGMAN SIMPLIFIED ENGLISH SERIES

Pride and Prejudice
Jane Austen
The Coral Island
R. M. Ballantyne
Best Short Stories of
Thomas Hardy
A Book of Shorter
Stories
British and American
Short Stories
Jane Eyre
Charlotte Brontë
Wuthering Heights
Emily Brontë
The 39 Steps
John Buchan
The Good Earth
Pearl Buck
The Moonstone
Wilkie Collins
The Woman in White
Wilkie Collins
The Hound of the
Baskervilles
Sir Arthur Conan Doyle
Hatter's Castle
A. J. Cronin
The Citadel
A. J. Cronin
The Stars Look Down
A. J. Cronin
Taste and other Tales
Roald Dahl
The Pickwick Papers
Charles Dickens
A Tale of Two Cities
Charles Dickens
The Three Musketeers
Alexandre Dumas
Frenchman's Creek
Daphne du Maurier
Jamaica Inn
Daphne du Maurier

Rebecca
Daphne du Maurier
Further Detective
Stories
Doctor in the House
Richard Gordon
Great American
Detective Stories
Airport
Hotel
Arthur Hailey
Far from the Madding
Crowd
Thomas Hardy
The Prisoner of Zenda
Anthony Hope
Campbell's Kingdom
Hammond Innes
Three Men in a Boat
Jerome K. Jerome
Tales from Shakespeare
More Tales from
Shakespeare
Charles and Mary Lamb
Sons and Lovers
D. H. Lawrence
Call for the Dead
John le Carré
Moby Dick
Herman Melville
Kojak: The Trade-Off
Victor B. Miller
Modern American Short
Stories
Mystery Stories
Outstanding Short
Stories
Shaka Zulu
E. A. Ritter
Jaws 2
Hank Searls
Sherlock Holmes Short
Stories

Short Stories of D. H.
Lawrence
Spinechillers
The Strange Case of Dr
Jekyll and Mr Hyde
Kidnapped
R. L. Stevenson
Castle of Danger
Mary Stewart
Stories of Detection and
Mystery
Summer Romance and
Other Short Stories
Tales of Mystery and
Imagination
Vanity Fair
W. M. Thackeray
The Adventures of
Huckleberry Finn
The Adventures of Tom
Sawyer
Mark Twain
2001 and Beyond
Journey to the Centre of
the Earth
Round the World in 80
days
Jules Verne
The Invisible Man
H. G. Wells
The Wooden Horse
Eric Williams
Roller Coaster
Burton Wohl
The Kraken Wakes
John Wyndham

JAMAICA INN

by

DAPHNE DU MAURIER

ABRIDGED AND SIMPLIFIED BY
ALAN RONALDSON M.A.

Illustrated by Eric Thomas

LONGMAN

Longman Group UK Limited
Longman House, Burnt Mill
Harlow, Essex CM20 2JE, England
and Associated Companies throughout the world.

*First Published in this series 1962
by arrangement with Victor Gollancz Ltd
Sixty-seventh impression 1990*

*Produced by Longman Group (FE) Ltd.
Printed in Hong Kong*

ISBN 0-582-52823-2

Longman Simplified English Series

This book has been specially prepared to make enjoyable reading for people to whom English is a second or a foreign language. An English writer never thinks of avoiding unusual words, so that the learner, trying to read the book in its original form, has to turn frequently to the dictionary and so loses much of the pleasure that the book ought to give.

This series is planned for such readers. There are very few words used which are outside the learner's vocabulary[1]. These few extra words are needed for the story and are explained when they first appear. Long sentences and difficult sentence patterns have been simplified. The resulting language is good and useful English, and the simplified book keeps much of the charm and flavour of the original.

At a rather more difficult level there is *The Bridge Series*, which helps the reader to cross the gap between the limited vocabulary and structures of the *Simplified English Series* and full English.

It is the aim of these two series to enable thousands of readers to enjoy without great difficulty some of the best books written in the English language, and in doing so, to equip themselves in the pleasantest possible way, to understand and appreciate any work written in English.

[1] The 2,000 root words of the *General Service List of English Words* of the *Interim Report on Vocabulary Selection*.

INTRODUCTION

Daphne du Maurier is the daughter of Sir Gerald du Maurier, who was a popular English actor. In 1934 she wrote a successful book about him, *Gerald, A Portrait*. Since then she has written other books about her famous family. She is married to Sir Frederick Browning, who was a distinguished soldier and is now Treasurer to the Duke of Edinburgh. They live in a fine old house beside the sea in Cornwall.

One of Daphne du Maurier's most popular books, *Rebecca*, was about such a house. *Frenchman's Creek* was also about the Cornish coast. Both these books were made into films.

Jamaica Inn was written in 1935. This lonely inn stands on the highroad in a wild and empty part of Cornwall, and many names in the book are those of real places. But the story itself is imaginary. It tells of the Cornwall of a hundred and fifty years ago, when travel was slow and visitors were few. No police force existed, and it was hard to make some of the wild and cruel people keep the law. As Mary Yellan discovers in this story, some of them had strange ways of making a living . . .

The story of her life at Jamaica Inn is full of adventure, and makes this one of Daphne du Maurier's most exciting books.

1

IT was a cold grey day in late November, and although it was now only a little after two o'clock in the afternoon the dark of a winter evening seemed to have come down upon the hills, hiding them in cloud. The air was cold, and in spite of the tightly closed windows it came into the coach.[1] The leather seats felt damp to the hands, and there must have been a small crack in the roof, because now and again little drops of rain fell softly through, leaving on the leather a dark-blue stain like a mark made by ink. The wind blew hard. The wheels of the coach sank into the holes in the road, and sometimes they threw up mud against the windows, where it mixed with the rain so that any view there might have been was blocked out.

The few passengers sat close together for warmth. Mary Yellan sat where the drops of rain came through the crack in the roof. She brushed them away with impatient fingers. Although she was hardly forty miles by road from what had been her home for twenty-three years, the hope within her heart had tired. The courage which was so large a part of her, and had helped her so much during the long misery of her mother's illness and death, was now shaken by this rain and wind.

She remembered the letter from her aunt. The writer said that the news from her niece had given her a shock; that she had had no idea that her sister was ill, because it was many years since she had been to her home in Helford. And she went on: "There have been changes with us that you would not know. I no longer live in Bodmin, but nearly twelve miles outside it, on the road to Launceston. It's a wild and lonely spot, and if you were to come to us I should be glad of your

---

[1] *coach*—large four-wheeled carriage for passengers, drawn by horses.

1

company in winter-time. I have asked your uncle, and he does not object, he says, if you do not talk too much and will give help when it is needed. He cannot give you money or feed you for nothing, as you will understand. He will expect your help in the bar[1] in return for your board and lodging. You see, your uncle is the landlord of Jamaica Inn."

Mary folded the letter. It was a strange message of welcome from the smiling Aunt Patience she remembered. A cold, empty letter, giving no word of comfort, and admitting nothing, except that her niece must not ask for money. Aunt Patience, with her silk skirts and delicate ways, the wife of an inkeeeper!

So it was that Mary Yellan found herself travelling northward in the coach. Villages were scattered now, and there were few smiling faces at the cottage doors. Trees were few. The wind blew and the rain came with the wind. And so the coach rolled into Bodmin, grey and unwelcoming like the hills around it, and one by one the passengers gathered up their things ready to leave—all except Mary, who sat still in her corner. The driver, his face a stream of rain, looked in at the window.

"Are you going on to Launceston?" he said. "It'll be a wild drive tonight across the moors.[2] You can stay in Bodmin, you know, and go on by coach in the morning. There'll be no one in this coach going on but you."

"My friends will be expecting me," said Mary. "I'm not afraid of the drive. And I don't want to go as far as Launceston; will you please stop for me at Jamaica Inn?"

The man looked at her curiously. "Jamaica Inn?" he said. "What would you do at Jamaica Inn? That's no place for a girl. You must have made a mistake, surely?" He looked hard at her, not believing her. He called over his shoulder to a woman who stood in the doorway of the Royal Hotel, lighting a lamp. It was already getting dark.

"Come here and reason with this young girl. I was told

---

[1] *bar*—room in an inn where drinks are served.
[2] *moors*—wide spaces of hilly waste land.

she was going to Launceston, but she has asked me to leave her at Jamaica Inn!"

The woman came down the steps and looked into the coach.

"It's a wild, rough place up there," she said, "and if you're looking for work, you won't find it on the farms. They don't like strangers on the moors. You'd do better down here in Bodmin."

Mary smiled at her. "I shall be all right," she said. "I'm going to relatives. My uncle is the landlord of Jamaica Inn."

There was a long silence. In the grey light of the coach Mary could see that the woman and the man were looking at her. She felt cold, suddenly, and anxious. Then the woman drew back from the window. "I'm sorry," she said. "It's not my business, of course. Good night."

The driver began to whistle, rather red in the face, as one who wishes to end an awkward situation. Mary leant forward and touched his arm. "Would you tell me?" she said. "I shan't mind what you say. Is my uncle not liked? Is something the matter?"

The man looked very uncomfortable. He avoided her eyes. "Jamaica Inn's got a bad name," he said; "strange stories are told—you know how it is. But I don't want to make any trouble. Perhaps they're not true."

"What sort of stories?" asked Mary. "Do you mean that there is too much heavy drinking there? Does my uncle encourage bad company?"

The man would not say. "I don't want to make trouble," he repeated, "and I don't know anything. It's only what people say. Good people don't go to Jamaica Inn any more. That's all I know. In the old days we used to give the horses water there, and feed them, and go in for a bite of food and drink. But we don't stop there any more."

"Why don't people go there? What is their reason?"

The man hesitated; it was as if he were searching for words.

"They're afraid," he said at last; and then he shook his head; he would say no more. He shut the door and climbed into his seat.

The coach rolled away down the street, past the safe and solid houses, the busy lights, the scattered people hurrying home for supper, their figures bent against the wind and rain. Now the horses were climbing the steep hill out of the town and, looking through the window at the back of the coach, Mary could see the lights of Bodmin fast disappearing, one by one, until the last was gone. She was now alone with the wind and the rain, and twelve long miles of bare moor between her and her journey's end. She sat in her corner, shaken from side to side by the coach. On either side of the road the country stretched away into space. No trees, no paths, no cottages, but mile after mile of bare moor, dark and empty, rolling like a desert land to the unseen horizon. No human being could live in this country, thought Mary, and remain like other people; the very children would be born twisted, like the blackened bushes, bent by the force of a wind that never stopped blowing. Their minds would be twisted too, their thoughts evil, living as they must amongst marsh[1] and granite,[2] rough bushes and hard stone.

At last she lifted the window and looked out. Ahead of her, at the top of a hill on the left, was some sort of building, standing back from the road. She could see tall chimneys in the darkness. There was no other house, no other cottage. If this was Jamaica Inn, it stood alone, unprotected from the winds. Mary gathered her wrap around her. The horses had been pulled to a stop and stood sweating under the rain, the steam coming from them in a cloud.

The driver climbed down from his seat, pulling her box down with him. He seemed hurried, and kept looking over his shoulder towards the house.

"Here you are," he said, "across the yard over there. If you hammer on the door they'll let you in. I must be going on, or I'll not reach Launceston tonight."

---

[1] *marsh*—low-lying ground so soft and wet that people and animals could sink into it.

[2] *granite*—a very hard and ancient kind of rock, common on the surface of the moors in Cornwall.

In a moment the coach was away down the road

In a moment the coach was away down the road, disappearing as if it had never existed, lost and swallowed up in the darkness.

Mary stood alone, with her box at her feet. She heard the sound of the door being unbarred in the dark house behind her, and then it was thrown open. A great figure walked into the yard, swinging a light from side to side.

"Who is it?" came a shout. "What do you want here?"

Mary stepped forward and looked up into the man's face. The light shone in her eyes, and she could see nothing.

"Oh, it's you, is it?" he said. "So you've come to us after all? I'm your uncle, Joss Merlyn, and I give you welcome to Jamaica Inn." He drew her into the shelter of the house, laughing, then shut the door and put the light upon a table in the passage. And they looked at each other face to face.

2

HE was a great man, nearly seven feet high, with a big face and a dark brown skin. His thick black hair hung down over his eyes and round his ears. He looked as if he had the strength of a horse, with immense, powerful shoulders, long arms that reached almost to his knees, and large hands. His nose was hooked, curving to a mouth that might have been perfect once but was now sunken and fallen, and there was still something fine about his great dark eyes, in spite of the lines about them. The best things left to him were his teeth, which were all good still, and very white, so that when he smiled they showed up clearly against the brown of his face, giving him the appearance of a hungry animal.

"So you are Mary Yellan," he said at last, towering above her, his head bent to observe her more closely, "and you've come all this way to look after your Uncle Joss. I call it very nice of you."

He laughed again, his laugh roaring through the house, acting like a whip on Mary.

"Where is my Aunt Patience?" she asked, looking around her in the dark passage, with its cold stone floor and narrow staircase. "Is she not expecting me, then?"

"Where's my Aunt Patience?" he copied her. Then he lifted his face to the stairs.

"Patience!" he roared, "what are you doing? Here's the girl arrived, crying for you. She's tired of the sight of me already."

There was a noise at the top of the stairs, and a footstep dragged. Down the stairs came a woman, shielding the light from her eyes. She wore a cap on her thin grey hair, which hung to her shoulders. Her eyes were large, as though they continuously asked a question, and she had a little habit of moving her mouth, now tightening her lips and now letting them go loose. She wore a faded striped skirt that had once been red and was now a pale pink, and over her shoulders was thrown a much-mended wrap. Mary watched her without speaking, full of sorrow. Was this poor creature the beautiful Aunt Patience of her dreams—dressed like this, and looking twenty years older?

The little woman came down the stairs and into the hall; she took Mary's hands in hers and looked closely into her face. "Have you really come?" she whispered. "It is my niece Mary Yellan, isn't it? My dead sister's child?"

Mary nodded, thanking God that her mother could not see her now. "Dear Aunt Patience," she said gently, "I'm glad to see you again. It's so many long years since you came to us at Helford."

The woman suddenly held her tightly, burying her head against her shoulder, and she began to cry, loudly and fearfully.

"Ah, stop that," shouted the husband, "what sort of welcome is this? What have you got to cry about, you fool? Can't you see the girl wants her supper? Get out to the kitchen and give her some meat and a drink."

Aunt Patience controlled herself. She led the way to yet another dark passage, and so into the kitchen where a low fire burned.

"You mustn't mind your Uncle Joss," she said, her manner changing suddenly to that of a dog that has been trained by continuous cruelty to unquestioning obedience and who, in spite of kicks and curses, will fight fiercely for his master. "Your uncle must be treated carefully, you know; he has his ways, and strangers don't understand him at first. He's a very good husband to me, and has been ever since we were married."

She talked on mechanically, going backwards and forwards across the stone-floored kitchen as she laid the table for supper. There was a footstep outside the door, and with a sinking heart Mary realised that Joss Merlyn had come downstairs again. He came into the room, and looked from one to the other. He pulled a chair from the wall, and crashed it against the table. He sat down heavily, and reaching for the loaf, cut himself a great piece of bread, which he pushed into his mouth, and called Mary to the table. "You need food, I can see that," he said, and carefully buttered the loaf. He cut a thin piece from it and then cut this into four quarters for her, the whole business very delicately done and quite different from his manner in serving himself—so much so that to Mary there was something almost frightening in the change from roughness to gentle care. It was as if there was some power in his fingers which turned them suddenly into skilful servants. It was unexpected.

"Patience," he said, "here's the key. Go and fetch me a bottle, for the Lord's sake—I've a thirst!"

In a few minutes his wife returned with the bottle, which she put in front of her husband, and while she finished her cooking he began drinking, kicking the leg of the table. Suddenly he struck the table with his hand, shaking the plates and cups; one fell to the ground and broke.

"I tell you what, Mary Yellan," he shouted, "I'm master in this house, and I want you to know it. You'll do as you're told, and help in the house and serve in the bar, and I'll not lay a finger on you. But, by God, if you open your mouth, I'll tame you until you eat out of my hand the same as your aunt there."

Mary faced him across the table. She held her hands below the table so that he should not see them tremble.

" I understand you," she said. " It doesn't matter to me what you do in the inn. I'll do my work in the house, and you'll have no cause to complain. But if you hurt my Aunt Patience in any way, I tell you this—I'll leave Jamaica Inn straight away, and I'll find the magistrate[1] and bring him here, and use the law against you; and then try to tame me if you like! "

Mary had turned very pale. She did not know it, but she had saved herself; her little show of courage made an effect on the man.

" That's very pretty," he said; " very prettily put indeed. Now we know just what sort of visitor we have. Scratch her, and she shows her teeth. All right, my dear; you and I are more alike than I thought. If we are going to play, we'll play together. I may have work for you at Jamaica one day, work that you've never done before. Man's work, Mary Yellan, where you play with life and death." Mary heard Aunt Patience beside her. " Oh, Joss," she whispered. " Oh, Joss, please! "

There was so much fear in her voice that Mary looked at her in surprise. Her uncle waved his hand impatiently.

" Get up to bed, Patience," he said. " I'm tired of your miserable face at my supper table. This girl and I understand each other."

The woman rose at once and went to the door, with a last helpless look of despair over her shoulder. They heard her go up the stairs. Joss Merlyn and Mary were alone. He pushed the empty glass away from him and folded his arms on the table.

" There's been one weakness in my life, and I tell you what it is. It's drink. It's a curse, and I know it. I can't stop myself. One day it will be the end of me, and a good thing too. Days

---

[1] *magistrate*—country gentleman who acted as an officer of the law.

go by and I don't touch more than a drop. And then I'll feel
the thirst come on me and I'll drink—drink for hours. I talk
then—talk until everything I've done is told to the four winds.
I've told you because I've already had too much and I can't
hold my tongue. But I've not lost control of my head. I've
not had enough to tell you why I live in this God-forgotten
place, and why I'm the landlord of Jamaica Inn." His voice
was hardly more than a whisper. The fire had sunk low, and
dark shadows stretched long fingers on the wall. The light
cast a great shadow of Joss Merlyn on the roof. "The coaches
don't stop here now, nor the mails either. I don't worry; I've
visitors enough. The farther the gentlemen keep away, the
better pleased I am. Ah, there's drinking here all right, and
plenty of it too. There are some who come to Jamaica Inn
on Saturday night, and there are some who turn the key of
their door and sleep with their fingers in their ears. There are
nights when every cottage on the moors is dark and silent,
and the only lights for miles are the windows of Jamaica Inn.
They say the shouting and the singing can be heard as far
down as the farms below Roughtor. You'll be in the bar those
nights, if you like, and you'll see what company I keep."

Mary sat very still, holding hard to the sides of her chair.

"They're all afraid of me," he went on; "the whole damned
lot of them. Afraid of me, who's afraid of no man. It's the
drink that's been against me. Drink and my hot blood. It's the
curse of all of us, Mary. There's never been a Merlyn yet that
died peaceful in his bed.

"My father was hanged at Exeter—he had a quarrel with
a fellow, and killed him. I'm the eldest of three brothers, all
born under the shadow of Kilmar. You walk out over there
across the moor, and you will see a great rock of granite like
a devil's hand sticking up into the sky. That's Kilmar. If
you'd been born under its shadow you'd start to drink, as I
did. My brother Matthew was drowned in Trewartha Marsh.
We thought he had gone to be a sailor, and had no news of
him, and then in the summer no rain fell for seven months,
and there was Matthew sticking up in the marsh, with his

hands above his head, and the birds flying round him. My brother Jem was the baby. Hanging on to mother's skirts when Matthew and I were grown men. I never did agree with Jem. Too clever he is—too quick with his tongue. Oh, they will catch him in time and hang him, as they did my father."

He was silent, looking into his empty glass. "I've said enough. I'll have no more tonight. Go up to bed, Mary. You'll find your room above the front door."

Mary was about to pass him when he seized hold of her shoulder and twisted her round.

"There'll be nights sometimes when you hear wheels on the road," he said, "and those wheels will not pass on, but they'll stop outside Jamaica Inn. And you'll hear footsteps in the yard, and voices beneath your window. When that happens, you'll stay in bed, Mary Yellan, and cover your head with the bedclothes. Do you understand?"

"Yes, uncle."

"Very well. Now go, and if you ever ask me a question again I'll break every bone in your body."

She went out of the room and into the dark passage, and so upstairs, feeling the wall with her hands. Her uncle had told her that her room was over the front door. Her box lay on the floor. The walls were rough and the floorboards bare. A box turned upside down served as a table, with a cracked looking-glass on top. The bedclothes felt damp to her hand. She went to the window and looked out. The wind had gone down, but it was still raining—a thin, miserable rain that ran down the side of the house and mixed with the dirt on the window.

Whatever she would have to face in the future, and however frightened she would be, she would not leave Jamaica Inn now. She must stay with Aunt Patience. She was needed here. And so Mary lay upon her hard bed, her mind working while she prayed for sleep. She counted the minutes and the hours of an endless night, and when the first bird sang in the field behind the house she counted no more, but slept like a dead thing.

3

MARY woke to a high wind from the west, and a watery sun.

During the morning there was the usual work of the house, and Mary was thus able to explore the inn more thoroughly. It was a dark place, with long passages and unexpected rooms. There was a separate entrance to the bar, at the side of the house, and, though the room was empty now, there was something heavy in the air from the last time it was full—a taste of old tobacco, the sour smell of drink and of warm, unclean humanity crowded one against the other on the dark, stained wooden seats. Down a passage in the opposite direction from the kitchen, was another room, the door of which was locked. Mary went out into the yard to look at it through the window, but there was a board nailed up against the frame, and she could not see inside. The house and other buildings formed three sides of the square that was the little yard. Beyond this lay the road, a thin white ribbon that stretched to the horizon, surrounded on each side by the moors, brown and wet from the heavy rains. Mary went out on the road and looked round her, and as far as the eye could see there was nothing but the black hills and the moors. The grey stone inn, with its tall chimneys, was the only house in view.

She went back into the house to find Aunt Patience.

"Aunt Patience," she began, "why is my uncle the landlord of Jamaica Inn?" The sudden direct attack took the woman by surprise, and for a moment she looked back at Mary without reply. Then she went red. "Why," she said, "it's a very important place here, on the road. You can see that. This is the main road from the south. The coaches pass here twice a week. We do good trade here."

"How can you say that, when the rooms are never used, and the bedrooms are fit only for rats and mice? I've seen them for myself."

12

Her aunt was silent for a moment, working her mouth and twisting her fingers together. "Your Uncle Joss doesn't encourage people to stay. We do a good trade. I've told you that. Men come in from the farms. There are farms and cottages scattered all over the moors for miles around, and men come from there. There are evenings when the bar is full of them."

"The driver of the coach yesterday said that good people did not come to Jamaica any more. He said they were afraid."

Aunt Patience changed colour. She was pale now, and her eyes moved from side to side. She swallowed, and passed her tongue over her lips.

"Your Uncle Joss has a strong temper," she said; "you have seen that for yourself. He is easily angered; he will not have people interfering with him."

Her eyes begged to be excused further questioning and her face was pale. Mary saw that she had suffered enough, but risked one question more.

"Aunt Patience," she said, "I want you to look at me and answer me this, and then I won't worry you again. What has the barred room at the end of the passage to do with the wheels that stop outside Jamaica Inn by night?"

As soon as she had spoken she was sorry. A strange expression crept upon the woman's face, and her great hollow eyes looked across the table in fear. Her mouth trembled, and her hand wandered to her throat.

Mary pushed back her chair and knelt by her side. She put her arms around Aunt Patience, and held her close, and kissed her hair.

"I'm sorry," she said. "Don't be angry with me. It's not my business, and I've no right to question you, and I'm ashamed of myself. Please, please forget what I said."

Her aunt buried her face in her hands. Then she looked over her shoulder, as if she were afraid that Joss himself stood in the shadows behind the door.

"There are things happen at Jamaica Inn, Mary, that I've never dared to breathe a word about. Bad things. Evil things. I dare not even admit them to myself. Some of it in time you'll come to know. You can't avoid it, living here. Your Uncle Joss mixes with strange men, who follow a strange trade. Sometimes they come by night, and from your window you will hear footsteps, and voices, and knocking at the door. Your uncle lets them in, and he takes them along the passage to that room with the locked door. Before day they are gone, and no sign is left that they have ever been. When they come, Mary, you will say nothing to me or to your Uncle Joss. You must lie in bed and put your fingers to your ears."

Then she rose from the table, and pushed aside her chair, and Mary heard her climb the stairs with heavy feet.

Joss Merlyn was away from the house for nearly a week, and during that time Mary learnt something about the country. After helping her aunt in the house and kitchen, she was free to wander where she pleased.

The moors were even wilder than she had at first supposed. Like an immense desert they rolled from east to west, with paths here and there across the surface, and great hills standing up against the sky. It was a silent, empty country, untouched by human hand; on the high tors[1] the stones leant against one another in strange shapes, great watchmen who had stood there since the hand of God first made them. Wild sheep lived on the high tors. Black cattle fed on the moors beneath, their careful feet choosing the firm ground, as with inborn knowledge they avoided the long, tempting grass that was not grass at all, but soft marsh that invited. There was a silence on the tors that belonged to another age; an age that is past and gone as though it had never been, an age when man did not exist.

One day she crossed the East Moor, in the direction that Joss had given her the first evening; and when she had gone some way and stood alone upon a hill, surrounded on all sides by bare moors, she saw that the land sloped down to a deep and dangerous marsh, through which ran a stream. And rising

---

[1] *tor*—steep hill rising from the moors in Cornwall; usually much of it is granite, with bare rocks at the top.

beyond the marsh, away on the other side, pointing its fingers to the sky, was a great rock like a split hand coming steeply out of the moor; its surface of granite looked as if it had been cut by an artist. So this was Kilmar Tor; and somewhere amongst the solid mass of stone Joss Merlyn had been born and his brother lived today. Below her in the marsh, Matthew Merlyn had been drowned.

Mary turned her back upon Kilmar, and began to run across the moor, nor did she stop until the marsh disappeared below the level of the hill, and the tor itself was hidden. She had come farther than she had intended, and the way home was long. It seemed an age before the last hill was conquered and behind her, and the tall chimneys of Jamaica Inn stood out before her above the winding road. As she crossed the yard she noticed with a sinking heart that the stable[1] door was open, and the horse was inside. Joss Merlyn had returned.

She opened the door as silently as possible, but it rubbed against the stone floor and made a complaining noise.

In a moment the landlord appeared. Mary started to go up the stairs to her room, when Joss called her. " Here," he said, " no hiding up there this evening. There will be work for you in the bar, beside your uncle. Don't you know what day of the week it is? "

Mary paused to think. She was losing count of time. Was it Monday's coach she had taken? That made today Saturday—Saturday night. At once she realised what Joss Merlyn meant. Tonight there would be company at Jamaica Inn.

4

THEY came singly, the people of the moors, crossing the yard quickly and silently, as if they had no wish to be seen. They were a strange group around Joss Merlyn in th

[1] *stable*—building in which horses are kept.

bar. Half hidden by a screen of bottles and glasses, Mary could look down on the company and remain unobserved. They lay on the seats; they leant against the walls; they sat beside the tables; and one or two, whose heads or stomachs were weaker than the rest, already lay at full length upon the floor. Most of them were dirty, with long hair and broken finger-nails, cattle-stealers, wanderers and thieves. The smell of drink and tobacco and unwashed bodies was strong. Mary felt disgust rise up in her, and she knew that she would give way to it if she stayed there long. The evening seemed endless, and Mary's one thought was of escape. The air was so thick with smoke and breath that it was hard to see across the room, and to her tired, half-closed eyes the faces of the men seemed immense, all hair and teeth, their mouths much too large for their bodies, while those who had drunk too much lay on the seats or on the floor like dead men.

Those who could still stand had crowded round a dirty little pedlar[1] from Redruth, who had made himself the joker of the gathering. The tin-mine where he had worked was now in ruins, and he had become a pedlar, and had stored up a collection of songs with which he now entertained the company. The laughter that greeted his coarse jokes nearly shook the roof. To Mary there was something horrible in this ugly, shouting laughter, which in some strange way held no note of amusement, but rang down the dark stone passages and into the empty rooms above like a despairing thing. Mary could bear it no longer. She touched her uncle on the shoulder, and he turned to her, his face red with the heat of the room and streaming with sweat.

"I can't bear this any more," she said. "You'll have to attend to your friends yourself. I'm going upstairs to my room."

"Had enough of it, have you? Think yourself too good for us? Get out, then; it's nearly midnight, in any case, and I don't want you. You'll lock your door tonight, Mary. Your

[1] pedlar—man who walks about from house to house selling things from a bag he carries on his back.

aunt's been in bed for an hour with the bedclothes over her head."

He lowered his voice; bending down to her ear and seizing her wrist, he twisted it behind her back, until she cried out in pain.

"Keep your mouth shut and I'll treat you gently. It is unwise to be curious at Jamaica Inn, and I wish you to remember that."

Mary ran out of the room, shutting the door hard behind her, and as she went up the stairs, her hand over her ears, she could not keep out that sound of laughter and wild song that sounded down the empty passage, following her to her room and even coming up through the cracks between the floor boards. Then she did as her uncle had told her. She undressed hurriedly and crept into bed, pulling the bedclothes over her head and putting her fingers in her ears, her only thought now to be deaf to the noise below.

She slept. Then, without warning, she was suddenly awake, sitting up in bed, with the moonlight streaming in upon her face. She listened, hearing nothing at first but the beating of her own heart, but in a few minutes there came another sound, from beneath her room this time—the sound of heavy things being dragged along the stone floor in the passage downstairs.

She got out of bed and went to the window. Five waggons[1] were drawn up in the yard outside. Three were covered, each drawn by a pair of horses, and the remaining two were open farm-carts. One of the covered waggons stood directly beneath the window, and the horses were steaming. Gathered round the waggons were some of the men who had been drinking in the bar earlier in the evening. And there were strangers in the yard whom Mary had never seen before. She began to understand. Packages were brought by the waggons and unloaded at Jamaica Inn. They were stored in the locked room. All was done in silence. Those men who had shouted and sung earlier that night were now quiet, Joss Merlyn came out of the front door, the pedlar at his side.

[1] *waggon*—big four-wheeled farm cart, in which horses pull heavy loads.

" Is that the lot? " he called softly, and the driver of the last waggon waved and held up his hand. So the waggons and carts moved away from Jamaica, rolling out of the yard one after another, some turning north and some south when they came out on to the road, until they had all gone, and there was no one left standing in the yard but one man whom Mary had not seen before, the pedlar, and the landlord of Jamaica Inn himself. Then they, too, turned and went back into the house. She heard them go along the passage in the direction of the bar, and a door closed. There was no other sound except that of the big clock in the hall. It rang the hour— three o'clock.

Mary came away from the window and sat down upon the bed. The cold air blew in upon her shoulders, and she trembled. This was smuggling[1] on a grand scale. Had Joss Merlyn the necessary brain to head such a business? Had he been making preparations for tonight's work during the past week, when away from home? The agents must be carefully picked, in spite of their wild appearance, and the whole business controlled, or the law could never have been broken for so long. A magistrate who suspected smuggling would surely have suspected the inn—unless he were an agent himself. If it were not for Aunt Patience she would walk out of the inn now, find her way to the nearest town and give information about Joss Merlyn. He would soon be in prison, and the rest of them with him, and there would be an end to the trade.

But had she seen only part of the business, and was there still more for her to learn? She remembered the fear in Aunt Patience's eyes, and those words spoken when the shadows crept across the kitchen floor: " There are things happen at Jamaica Inn, Mary, that I've never dared to breathe a word about. Bad things. Evil things. I dare not even admit them to myself." And she had climbed the stairs to her room, dragging her feet like a creature old and tired. Smuggling was dangerous; it was not honest; it was strictly forbidden by the

---

[1] *smuggling*—bringing goods into a country secretly, without paying money to the government.

law; but was it evil? Mary needed advice, and there was no
one she could ask. Here she was, a girl of twenty-three, with
no weapons but her own brain to fight a fellow twice her size
and eight times her strength.

"I'll not show fear before Joss Merlyn or any man," she
said. "I will go down now and take a look at them in the
bar, and if they kill me it will be my own fault."

She dressed hurriedly, and then, opening the door, she
stood and listened for a moment, hearing nothing but the
sound of the clock in the hall. She crept out into the passage,
and came to the stairs. By now she knew that the third step
from the top would make a noise, and so would the last. She
stepped gently, and so she came to the dark hall by the front
door, empty except for one unsteady chair and the shadowy
outline of the great clock.

As she hesitated, a sudden beam of light shone into the
passage, and she heard voices. The door of the bar had swung
open. The men must be sitting on the seats against the outside
wall, because she could not see them. They had fallen to
silence. Then suddenly a man's voice rang out, trembling and
high, the voice of a stranger.

"No, and no again. I tell you for the last time. I'll have
no part in it. I'll break with you now and for ever, and put
an end to the agreement. That's murder you want me to do,
Mr. Merlyn; there's no other. name for it; it's common
murder."

Someone—the landlord himself no doubt—made reply in
a low voice. Mary could not catch his words, but his speech
was broken by a burst of laughter that she recognised as
belonging to the pedlar.

He must have asked a question. "Hanging, is it? I've risked
hanging before, and I'm not afraid for my neck. No, I'm thinking of my conscience. When it comes to the killing of harmless
people, and perhaps women and children among them, that's
wicked, Joss Merlyn, and you know it as well as I do."

Mary heard the scraping of a chair, and the man rising to
his feet; then her uncle lifted his voice for the first time.

"Not so fast my friend," he said, "not so fast! You're in this business as far as you can be. I tell you there's no going back now; it's too late; too late for you and for all of us. I've been doubtful of you from the first, with your gentleman's ways and your clean shirts, and by God I've proved myself right. Harry, fasten the door over there and put the bar across it."

There was a sudden cry, and the noise of someone falling, and at the same time the table crashed to the floor. Once more the pedlar laughed, and he began to whistle one of his songs.

"Harry, stand where you are by the door, and touch him with your knife if he tries to pass you. Now, look here, Mr. Lawyer-Clerk, you've made a fool of yourself tonight, but you're not going to make a fool of me. You'd like to walk out of that door, wouldn't you, and get on your horse, and ride away to Bodmin? Yes, and by nine in the morning you'd have every magistrate in the country at Jamaica Inn, and a party of soldiers as well. That's your fine idea, isn't it?"

Mary could hear the stranger breathe heavily, and he must have been hurt, for when his voice came it was sharp. "Do your devil's work if you must. I can't stop you, and I give you my word that I'll not give information about you. But join you I will not, and there's my last word to you both."

There was a silence, and then Joss Merlyn spoke again. "Take care," he said softly. "I heard another man say that once, and five minutes later he was walking the air. On the end of a rope it was, my friend, and his big toe missed the floor by half an inch. I asked him if he liked to be so near the ground, but he didn't answer. They said afterwards that he had taken seven minutes to die."

Outside in the passage, Mary felt herself go cold with sweat and her arms and legs were suddenly as heavy as lead. With a growing sense of fear she realised that she was probably going to faint.

Her uncle's voice came from very far away. "Leave me alone with him, Harry," he said. "There'll be no more work for you tonight at Jamaica. Take his horse and go. I'll settle this business by myself."

Somehow Mary found her way down the passage, and hardly knowing what she was doing, she turned the handle of a door and fell inside.

She must have fainted and have been unconscious for a minute or two, but then she sat up, listening to the sound of a horse in the yard outside. It was Harry the pedlar. Then a sound from above made her lift her head. It was the noise of a floorboard. Then it happened again: quiet footsteps above. Mary's heart began to beat faster, and her breath came quickly. Whoever was hiding up above must have been there many hours. He must have hidden so that he should remain unseen by the smugglers. Someone—a friend perhaps—was hiding in the room next to her bedroom, and could help her to save the stranger in the bar.

But as she waited, trembling, she heard the landlord pass across the hall and climb the stairs. His footsteps stopped above her head. Then he knocked, very softly, on the door. Once more the floorboard made a noise as someone crossed the floor, and the door was opened. Mary's heart sank within, and her despair returned. Her uncle had known him to be there all the time, and that was why he had sent the pedlar away. He did not wish the pedlar to see his friend. Now they were coming down the stairs; they stopped for an instant outside the door of the room which Mary had entered. For one moment she thought that they were coming inside. They were so close to her that she could have touched her uncle on the shoulder through the crack of the door. Then he spoke, and his voice whispered right against her ear.

" You must say. It's your judgement now, not mine. I'll do it, or we'll do it between us. It's you who must say the word."

Hidden as she was by the door, Mary could neither see nor hear her uncle's new companion, and whatever sign he made in reply remained unknown to her. They did not stay outside the room, but went off down the passage to the bar. Then the door closed, and she heard them no more.

Her first desire was to run out into the road, and so away
from them; but she soon realised that by doing that she would
gain nothing; quite possibly there might be other men on
guard along the high road in case of trouble. She must have
stood for ten minutes or more waiting for some sound or
signal, but everything was still. Only the clock in the hall
went on. Then she went out into the dark passage. No crack
of light came out under the door to the bar. She laid her ear
against it. There was no sound. Through the keyhole came a
steady current of cold air. Mary gave way to a sudden idea;
she opened the door and stepped into the room.

There was nobody there. The door leading to the yard was
open, and the room was filled with fresh November air. The
seats were empty, and the table that had crashed to the ground
still lay upon the floor, its legs pointing to the roof.

A last little ray of moonlight made a white circle on the
floor, and into the circle moved a dark shape like a finger. It
was a shadow. Mary looked up and saw that a rope had been
thrown over a hook in a beam. It was the rope's end that
made the shadow in the circle; and it kept moving backwards
and forwards, blown by the wind from the open door.

5

AS the days passed, Mary Yellan settled down to life at
Jamaica with a sense of determination. It was clear that
she could not leave her aunt to go through the winter alone;
she must make the best of the six months that lay ahead. If
possible, she was determined to defeat her uncle and deliver
him and his companions to the law. The events of that first
Saturday night were never far from her mind, and the meaning of the rope's end hanging from the beam was clear. Mary
had not a doubt that the stranger had been killed by her
uncle and another man, and his body buried somewhere on

the moors. There was nothing to prove it, however, and in the light of day the story seemed impossible.

Two weeks went by, and there was no Saturday night like it. No one came to the inn. The future seemed very black at times, especially as Aunt Patience made little effort to be a companion; and though now and again she took hold of Mary's hand, telling her how glad she was to have her in the house, most of the time the poor woman existed in a dream, going about her household duties in a mechanical way and seldom speaking.

One morning Mary set herself to clean down the long stone passage that ran the full width of the back of the house. Soon she heard the noise of a horse in the yard, and in a moment someone thundered on the closed door of the bar.

No one had come near Jamaica Inn before, and this was an event itself. Mary wiped her hands and went into the bar. There was a man sitting across a chair, with a glass in his hand which he had calmly filled for himself. For a few minutes they considered each other in silence. Something about him was familiar, and Mary wondered where she had seen him before. The heavy eyelids, the curve of his mouth, and the outline of his jaw, even the bold look which he gave her, were things known to her and disliked. The sight of him examining her and drinking at the same time angered her.

"What do you think you're doing?" she said. "You haven't any right to walk in here and help yourself."

The man finished his drink, and held out his glass to be refilled.

"Since when have they kept a barmaid[1] at Jamaica Inn?" he asked her, and, feeling in his pocket for a pipe, he lit it, blowing a great cloud of smoke in her face. His manner angered Mary, and she leant forward and pulled the pipe out out of his hand, throwing it behind her on to the floor, where it broke at once.

"Is this how they train you to serve your guests? I haven't

---
[1] *barmaid*—woman who serves in the bar of an inn.

a high opinion of their choice. Fill up my glass! That's what you're here for, isn't it?" he said.

"As you seem to know your way about here, you can fill your own glass. I'll tell Mr. Merlyn you are in the bar, and he can serve you himself if he likes."

"Oh, don't worry Joss. What's happened to his wife? Has he sent her away to make room for you? I call that unkind to the poor woman!"

"Do you want to speak to the landlord or not? I can't stand here all day. If you don't want to see him, and you have finished your drink, you can put your money on the table and go away."

The man laughed. "Do you give orders to Joss in that way?" he said. "He must be a changed man if you do."

"Joss Merlyn is my uncle by marriage," she said. "My name is Mary Yellan, if that means anything to you. Good morning. There's the door behind you."

She left the bar, meeting the landlord himself at the door.

"Oh, it's you, Jem, is it? What do you want at Jamaica Inn?" He closed the door, leaving Mary in the passage outside.

She went back to her bucket of water in the front hall. So that was Jem Merlyn, her uncle's younger brother. Of course he had reminded her of her uncle all through the conversation, though she had not realised it. He had Joss Merlyn's eyes, without the lines round them, and he had Joss Merlyn's mouth, firm, though, where the landlord's was weak. He was what Joss Merlyn might have been eighteen or twenty years ago—but smaller in build, and neater. This Jem had the same cruelty as his brother—she could see it in the shape of his mouth. Aunt Patience had said he was the worst of the family.

She was so busy that she did not hear the stone thrown at the window of the room, and it was not until a shower of little stones cracked the glass that, looking out of the window, she saw Jem Merlyn standing in the yard beside his horse.

Mary unfastened the heavy entrance door and went out.

"What do you want now?" she asked him.

" Oh, it's you, Jem, is it? "

"Forgive me if I was rude to you just now," he said.
"Somehow I didn't expect to see a woman at Jamaica Inn—
not a young girl like you, anyway. I know I deserve black
looks for looking at you as I did, but if you knew my brother
as well as I do you'd understand how I made the mistake. It
looks strange, having a girl at Jamaica Inn. Why did you
come here in the first place?"

He looked serious now, and his likeness to Joss had gone
for the moment. She wished he were not a Merlyn.

"I came here to be with my Aunt Patience," she said. "My
mother died some weeks ago, and I have no other relative. I'll
tell you one thing, Mr. Merlyn—I am thankful my mother
isn't alive to see her sister now."

"You haven't a good opinion of the landlord, then?"

"No, I have not," she replied. "He's turned my aunt from
a laughing, happy woman into a miserable slave, and I'll never
forgive him for that as long as I live."

"We Merlyns have never been good to our women. I can
remember my father beating my mother until she couldn't
stand. She never left him, though. When he was hanged at
Exeter she never spoke a word for three months. Her hair
went white with the shock. What she had to love in father I
can't say, for he never asked for her after he'd been taken,
and he left all his money to another woman the other side of
the river."

Mary was silent. The lack of feeling in his voice disgusted
her. She supposed that he had been born, like the rest of his
family, lacking the quality of tenderness.

"How long do you mean to stay at Jamaica?" he asked
suddenly. "There's not much company for you here."

"I'm not going away unless I take my aunt with me. I'd
never leave her alone, after what I have seen."

"What have you learnt, in your short time? It's quiet
enough here."

Mary thought that he might be trying to make her talk. It
was possible that her uncle had suggested that his brother
should speak to her, hoping in this way to obtain information.

" I helped my uncle in the bar one Saturday night, and I did not care for the company he kept."

" I don't suppose you did. The fellows who come to Jamaica have never been taught manners. They spend too much time in the county[1] prison."

" What do you do for a living? " asked Mary with sudden curiosity, for he spoke better than his brother.

" I'm a horse-thief," he said cheerfully, " but there's not much money in it, really. My pockets are always empty."

" Aren't you afraid of being caught? " said Mary.

" Thieving is an awkward thing to prove. Suppose a horse wanders away and his owner goes to look for him. These moors are full of wild horses and cattle. It's not going to be easy to find his horse. Say the pony had long hair, and one white foot, and a diamond mark in his ear. Off goes the owner to Launceston market with his eyes wide open. But he doesn't find his horse. It's there, of course. Only his hair is cut short, his four feet are all the same colour, and the mark in his ear is a square not a diamond. His owner doesn't look at him twice. That's simple enough, isn't it? "

Mary laughed, in spite of herself. He was so open in his dishonesty that she could not be angry with him.

Jem Merlyn looked at her seriously, and then he bent towards her, first looking quickly over her head into the door beyond.

" Look here," he said, " I'm serious now; you can forget all the nonsense I've told you. Jamaica Inn is no place for a girl —nor for any woman, if it comes to that. Why don't you run away? I would put you on the road to Bodmin."

Mary could almost have trusted him. But she could not forget that he was Joss Merlyn's brother, and, being that, might deceive her. Time would show whose side he was on.

" I don't need any help," she said. " I can look after myself."

Jem threw himself lightly on to his horse's back. " All right," he said. " I won't worry you. My cottage is the other

---

[1] *county*—a division of the country with its own local government; here, Cornwall.

side of Trewartha Marsh. I shall be there until the Spring, anyway. Good day to you." And he was off, and away down the road before she had time to say a word in reply.

Mary went slowly back into the house, and the cold, dead air of Jamaica Inn closed round her.

6

THAT night the waggons came again. This time they arrived empty, and were loaded with the last of the goods left at the inn the time before. Mary guessed that this was their way of working. The inn was used as a store for a few weeks at a time and then, when the opportunity came, the waggons set out once more, and the goods were carried to the river bank and sent to different places from there. The organisation must be a big one to move all the goods in the time, and there would be agents scattered far and wide who kept the necessary watch on events. It was with a sudden sting of disappointment that Mary wondered whether the visit of Jem Merlyn to Jamaica Inn this morning had been important. A strange thing that the waggons should follow him! He had come from Launceston, he said, and Launceston stood on the river bank. Mary was angry with him and with herself. In spite of everything, her last thought before sleeping had been the possibility of his friendship. She would be a fool if she had hopes of it now. The two events went together in a way which was quite clear. Jem might disagree with his brother, but they were both in the same trade. It was a miserable, wicked business in every way, and here she was in the middle of it all, with Aunt Patience like a child to be looked after.

The next few days passed in peace. Then there came a fine cold morning when for a change the sun shone in a cloudless sky. Mary, whose spirits always rose at the sight of the sun, had turned her morning into a washing-day; she felt well, and sang as she worked. Her uncle had ridden away on the moors somewhere, and a sense of freedom filled her whenever he was away.

An urgent tapping at the window made her look up, and she saw Aunt Patience making signs to her, very white in the face and clearly frightened. Mary wiped her hands and ran to the back door of the house.

" It's Mr. Bassat from North Hill," Aunt Patience whispered. " I saw him from the window. He's come on horseback, and another gentleman with him. Oh, my dear, my dear, what are we going to do? "

Mary thought quickly. She was in a very difficult position. If this was Mr. Bassat and he represented the law, it was her own chance of telling about her uncle. She could tell him of the waggons and of all that she had seen since her arrival. She looked down at the trembling woman at her side. The hammering on the door was continuous now.

" Mary, if Mr. Bassat asks you what you know, you won't answer him, will you? I can trust you, can't I? You'll not tell him of the waggons? If any danger came to Joss I'd kill myself, Mary."

There was no argument after that.

Mary unfastened the heavy entrance door. There were two men outside. One had rained the blows on the door. The other was a big fellow on the back of a fine horse. His face was brown and heavily lined; Mary judged him to be about fifty years of age.

" You don't hurry here, do you? " he called. " There doesn't seem to be much of a welcome for travellers. Is the landlord at home? "

" If you please, Mr. Bassat, my husband went out as soon as he had had his breakfast, and whether he will be back before night I cannot say."

" That's a nuisance. I wanted a word or two with Mr. Joss Merlyn." Mr. Bassat climbed heavily to the ground. " While I'm here I may as well look round, and I'll tell you here and now it's useless to refuse me. I am a magistrate, and I have the power." He pushed his way past the two women. Aunt Patience made a movement as though to prevent him, but Mary said quietly. "Let him go. If we try to stop him now we shall only anger him the more."

The rooms were thoroughly explored. The magistrate looked into the dusty corners, lifted the old bags, examined the stores of food, all the time crying out in anger and disgust. "Call this an inn, do you? Why you haven't even got a bed fit for a cat to sleep on. The place is rotten right through. What does it mean, eh? Have you lost your tongue, Mrs. Merlyn?"

The poor woman could not reply; she kept shaking her head and working her mouth, and Mary knew that she was wondering what would happen when they came to the barred room in the passage.

"What about you, young woman? Have you anything to say?'

"I'm here to look after my aunt. She's not very strong; you can see that for yourself. She's easily frightened."

"I don't blame her, living in a place like this. Well, kindly show me the room that has barred windows. I noticed it from the yard, and I'd like to see inside."

"I'm very sorry, sir," Mary replied, "but if you mean the old store room at the end of the passage, I'm afraid the door is locked. My uncle always keeps the key, and where he puts it I don't know."

"Well, that's easily settled. We'll have the door down in no time." He went out into the yard to call his servant. In a few minutes he returned with his man, Richards, who carried an old bar which he had found in the stable. For a few minutes the door resisted him. Then there was a splitting of wood and a crash, and the door gave way. It was dark of course; the blocked windows kept the light out. The servant produced a light, and the magistrate stepped into the room.

For a moment there was silence as the magistrate turned, letting the light shine in every corner, and then he turned to the little group behind him.

"Nothing," he said; "absolutely nothing. The landlord has made a fool of me again."

Except for a pile of empty bags in one corner, the room was completely bare. It was thick with dust. There was no furniture of any sort, the fire-place had been blocked up with stones and the floor was of stone like the passage outside. On top of the bags lay a length of twisted rope.

Then the magistrate turned once more into the passage.

"Well, Mr. Joss Merlyn has won this time. I'll admit myself beaten. Now listen to me," he said, pointing his whip at Mary. "This aunt of yours may have lost her tongue, but you can understand plain English, I hope. Do you mean to tell me you know nothing of your uncle's business? Does nobody ever call here, by day or night?"

Mary looked him straight in the eye. "I've never seen anyone," she said.

"Have you ever looked into that barred room before today?"

"No."

"Have you any idea why he should keep it locked up?"

"No, none at all."

"Have you ever heard wheels in the yard by night?"

"I'm a very heavy sleeper. Nothing ever wakes me."

"Where does your uncle go when he's away from home?"

"I don't know."

"Don't you think yourself it's very peculiar, to keep an inn on the main road, and then bar your house to every traveller?"

"My uncle is a very peculiar man."

"He is indeed. In fact, he's so very peculiar that half the people in the countryside won't sleep quietly in their beds until he's been hanged, like his father before him. You can tell him that from me." He climbed on to his horse. "One other thing," he called, from the saddle. "Have you seen anything of your uncle's younger brother, Jem Merlyn, of Trewartha?"

"No," said Mary steadily. "He never comes here."

"Oh, doesn't he? Well, that's all I want from you this

morning. Good day to you both." And away the two men
went from the yard, and so on to the road.

Joss Merlyn returned just before noon. Mary told him
calmly what had happened during the morning. He swore and
shouted, but he was frightened, she could see that, and his
confidence was shaken.

" Get me something to eat," he said. " I must go out again,
and there's no time to waste. You've done well today, Mary,
and I'll not forget it."

She looked him in the eyes. " You don't think I did it for
you, do you? "

" I don't care why you did it; the result's the same."

As soon as he had finished his meal, the landlord rose to
his feet and left the kitchen. Mary watched him cross the
moor. For a moment she hesitated, doubting the wisdom of
the sudden plan in her head, and then, seizing her thick
wrap, she ran down the field after her uncle. When she
reached the bottom, she bent down beside the stone wall until
his figure went over the hill and disappeared, and then she
jumped up again and followed him, picking her way amongst
the rough grass and stones. It was mad, no doubt, but her
idea was to keep Joss Merlyn in view, and in this way to
learn something of his secret plan. After a few miles she
realised how difficult it was. She had to keep a good distance
between them in order to remain unseen, and the landlord
walked at such a speed that before long she saw that she
would be left behind. The ground was now soft beneath her
feet; the whole of the low-lying plain before her was wet with
winter rains. Her uncle had crossed the worst of the low
ground with the quickness given by many years of practice.
Then he was hidden by a big rock of granite and she saw
him no more.

It was impossible to discover the path which he had taken
across the marsh, but Mary followed as best she could. She
was a fool to attempt it, she knew, but a sort of determined
stupidity made her continue. When she reached the top of the

hill the evening clouds were thick, and the world was grey. The horizon was hidden. Mary would never find her uncle now. She knew herself to be a fool for having gone so far on a December afternoon; experience had proved to her that when darkness came on Bodmin moor it was sudden and without warning. The low cloud over the marshes was dangerous too. But there was less danger from the marshes if she kept to the high ground, so, pulling up her skirt and holding her wrap closely round her shoulders, she walked steadily forward, feeling the ground with some care when in doubt, and avoiding those places where the grass felt soft and yielding to her feet. Her limbs were heavy dragging things that scarcely belonged to her, and her eyes felt sunken away back in her head. She walked on, her head low and her hands at her side, thinking that the tall grey chimneys of Jamaica Inn would be, for the first time, a welcome sight. The path was broader now, and was crossed by another running from left to right, and Mary stood uncertainly for a few moments, wondering which to take. It was then that she heard the sound of a horse coming out of the darkness to the left.

Mary waited in the middle of the track, and after some time the horse appeared out of the low cloud in front of her The horseman turned sharply aside as he saw Mary, and stopped.

"Hullo," he cried, "who's there? Is anyone in trouble?" Then, looking down closely from his saddle, he said in surprise, 'A woman! What in the world are you doing out here?"

"Can you help me to find the road? I'm miles from home and hopelessly lost."

"Steady there!" he said to his horse. "Stand still, will you? Where have you come from? Of course I will help you if I can." His voice was low and gentle.

"I live at Jamaica Inn," she said, and as soon as the words were out of her mouth she regretted them. For a moment the man was silent, but when he spoke again his voice had not changed, but was quiet and gentle as before.

" Jamaica Inn? " he said. " You've come a long way in the wrong direction, I'm afraid. You're tired out. You're not fit to walk another step; and what's more, I'm not going to let you. We are not far from the village, and you shall ride there. You shall come home with me, and dry those things and rest a little and have some supper, before I take you back myself to Jamaica Inn." He spoke with such kindness, and yet with such firmness, that Mary sighed with relief. Then she saw his eyes for the first time beneath the edge of his hat. They were strange eyes, like glass, and so pale in colour that they seemed near to white. His hair was white, too, under his black hat, and Mary looked at him in some surprise, because his face had no lines of age and his voice was not that of an old man.

Then, with sudden confusion, she understood, and she turned away her eyes. He was an albino.[1]

He took off his hat. " Perhaps I had better introduce myself. However unusual the meeting, it is the right thing to do I believe. My name is Francis Davey, and I am the vicar[2] of Altarnun.

7

THERE was something strangely peaceful about his house. Mary spread out her hands towards the fire. The silence pleased her. She watched Francis Davey as he laid the table for supper. " Hannah lives in the village," he said. " She leaves every afternoon at four. I prefer to be by myself. I like getting my own supper, and then I can choose my own time."

She could not yet accustom herself to his white hair and his eyes; his black clothes made them even more noticeable.

---

[1] *albino*—person who, lacking normal colouring matter in his body, has pale skin, white hair and almost colourless eyes.

[2] *vicar*—priest in charge of a church.

She was tired, but she swallowed her supper. He poured her out a steaming cup of tea. Now and again she took a quick look at him, but he seemed to feel it at once, for he would turn his eyes upon her with their cold white look like that of a blind man, and she would look away again. The warmth of the room and the hot tea made her sleepy, and his gentle voice came from far away.

"Why were you wandering on the moor tonight?"

Scarcely knowing how it happened, she heard her voice reply to his.

"I'm in terrible trouble," she said. "Sometimes I think I shall become like my aunt, and go out of my mind. I've not been at Jamaica Inn much more than a month, but it seems like twenty years. It's my aunt that worries me; if only I could take her away! But she won't leave Uncle Joss, in spite of his treatment of her. Every night when I go to bed I wonder if I shall wake up and hear the waggons. The first time they came, there were six or seven of them, and they brought great packages and boxes that the men stored in the barred room at the end of the passage. A man was killed that night; I saw the rope hanging from a beam downstairs. . . ." She stopped, the warm colour flooding her face. "I've never told anyone before. It had to come out. I couldn't keep it to myself any longer. I've done something terrible." For a moment or two he did not answer; then he spoke gently and slowly.

"Don't be afraid. Your secret is safe; no one shall know of this but me. When you have rested, I'll take you back, and I'll make your excuses to the landlord if you wish."

"Oh, you mustn't do that," said Mary quickly. "If he suspects half of what I have done tonight he would kill me, and you too. You don't understand. He's a violent man, and nothing would stop him."

"Isn't your imagination running away with you a little?" said the vicar. "This is the nineteenth century, you know, and men don't murder one another without reason. Having gone so far, don't you think you had better let me hear the rest of your story? What is your name, and how long have you been living at Jamaica Inn?"

Mary looked up at the pale eyes in the colourless face, at the crown of white hair, and she thought again how strange was this man, who might be twenty-one, who might be sixty, and who with his soft voice could persuade her to admit every secret she possessed, if he wanted to ask her. She could trust him; that at least was certain.

She started on her story with short and broken sentences, beginning with that first Saturday night at the bar, and then working backwards to her arrival at the inn. Her story did not sound true, even to her who knew the truth of it, and she was so tired that she often could not find the words, but paused for thought and then went back in her story and repeated herself. He heard her to the end with patience, but all the time she felt his white eyes watching her, and he had a little habit of swallowing from time to time which she came to recognise, and wait for.

When she had finished, the vicar got up from his chair and began to walk about the room.

"I believe you, of course," he said, after a moment or so, "but your story wouldn't be believed in a court of law. And another thing—it's wrong, we all know that, but smuggling goes on all over the country, and half the magistrates make a profit out of it. That surprises you, doesn't it? But you may be sure that it's the truth. I have met Mr. Bassat once or twice, and I believe him to be an honest sort of fellow, but, between ourselves, a bit of a fool. I can tell you one thing, though; his visit will have frightened your uncle. There won't be any more waggons to Jamaica Inn for some time; I think you can be certain of that. If I were you, I should just wait. Keep a close watch on your uncle, and when the waggons do come again you can tell me at once. We can then decide together what is best to be done."

"What about the stranger who disappeared? He was murdered. I'm certain of that. Do you mean to say that nothing can ever be done about it?"

" I'm afraid not, unless his body is found, which is extremely
unlikely," said the vicar. " In fact it's quite possible that he
was never killed at all. Forgive me, but I think you allowed
your imagination to run away with you over that. All you
saw was a piece of rope, remember. If you had actually seen
the man dead, or even wounded, well, that would be a different
matter altogether."

" I heard my uncle threaten him. Isn't that enough? "

" My dear child, people threaten one another every day in
the year, but they don't hang for it. Now listen to me. I am
your friend, and you can trust me. If you ever become worried
or frightened, I want you to come and tell me about it. Altarnun is only a few miles by the road. Now, that's agreed between
us, isn't it? "

" Thank you very much."

" Now I'm going to drive you back to Jamaica Inn."

The thought of returning was hateful to Mary, but it had
to be faced. The night was fine; the dark clouds of the early
evening had passed away and the sky was shining with stars.
It was a strange, exciting drive. The wind blew in Mary's
face. The horse thundered along the hard white road. The
vicar made no attempt to control it. He was smiling. " Go
on," he said, " go on; you can go faster than this," and his
voice was low and excited, as if he were talking to himself.
The effect was unnatural. Mary felt as if he were in another
world and had forgotten her existence. He looked like a bird,
bending forward in his seat; with his clothes blown by the
wind, his arms were like wings. He might be any age. Then
he smiled down at her, and was human again.

" I love these moors," he said. " If you knew them as well
as I do, and had seen them in every weather, winter and
summer, you would love them too. They go back a long way
in time. Sometimes I think that they have lived on from
another age. The moors were the first things to be made;
afterwards came the forests and the valleys and the sea."

Already Mary could see the tall chimneys of Jamaica Inn
outlined against the sky. The drive was ended, and the excite-

ment went from her. The old fear and hatred of her uncle
returned. The vicar stopped his horse just before the yard,
beside a grass bank.

"There's no sign of anyone," he said quietly. "It's like a
house of the dead. I am going to look in at the window."

She watched him go to the side of the house and he stood
there for a few minutes looking into the window. Then he
made a sign to her to follow. "There'll be no argument tonight
with the landlord of Jamaica Inn."

Mary followed the direction of his eyes and came forward
to the window. Joss Merlyn sat at the table unconscious, his
great legs stretched out on either side of him, his hat on the
back of his head. He looked straight in front of him at the
light, his eyes fixed like those of a dead man. A bottle lay
with its neck broken on the table, and beside it an empty
glass. The fire had burnt away to nothing.

Francis Davey pointed to the door. "You can walk inside
and go upstairs to bed. Your uncle will not even see you.
Good night to you, Mary Yellan. If you are ever in trouble
and need me, I shall be waiting for you at Altarnun." Then
he turned the corner of the house and was gone.

8

JOSS MERLYN was the worse for drink for five days.
He was unconscious most of the time, and lay stretched
out on a bed in the kitchen that Mary and her aunt had made
up. He slept with his mouth wide open, and the sound of his
breathing could be heard from the bedrooms above. About
five in the evening he would wake for about half an hour,
shouting for drink and crying like a child. His wife went to
him at once, talking to him gently, holding a glass to his lips
while he looked wildly around, talking to himself and
trembling like a dog. Aunt Patience became another woman,

Mary followed the direction of his eyes

showing a calm coolness which Mary would not have believed her to possess. It seemed that every two months or so Joss Merlyn would have these outbursts of drinking. They were becoming more frequent, and Aunt Patience was never quite certain when they would happen.

On the fifth morning the wind dropped and the sun shone, and in spite of the adventure of a few days before, Mary decided to try the moors again. This time she made for the East Moor, walking towards Kilmar. With many hours of daylight to come, there was no danger of being lost.

Mary had walked for an hour or more before she stopped, her further progress barred by a stream. It lay in a valley in the hills, and was surrounded by marshes. The country was not unknown to her; looking on beyond the green face of the tor ahead, she saw the great hand of Kilmar pointing its fingers to the sky. She was looking at Trewartha Moor once again, where she had wandered that first Saturday, but this time her face was turned to the south-east, and the hills looked different in the sunshine. The stream ran cheerfully over the stones. There was a gate lying across it as a bridge. As Mary crossed it, a group of horses came down the hill beyond and pushed into the stream to drink. Out of the corner of her eye she saw a man coming down the path, carrying a bucket in each hand. She was about to continue her walk round the bend of the hill when he waved a bucket in the air and shouted to her. It was Jem Merlyn. There was no time to escape, so she stood where she was until he came to her, looking just as his brother must have looked twenty years ago.

" So you've found your way to me, have you? " he said. " I didn't expect you so soon, or I've have baked some bread in your honour. I haven't washed for three days and I've been living on potatoes. Here, take hold of this bucket."

He pushed one of the buckets into her hand and ran down to the water after the horses. " Come out of it! " he shouted, "dirtying my drinking water. Go on, you big black devil."

He hit the largest of the horses with the end of the bucket, and they all ran up the hill out of the water, kicking their feet in the air.

" What would you have done if you hadn't found me at home? " he said, wiping his face on his arm. Mary could not help smiling.

" I didn't even know you lived here, and I certainly never walked this way with the intention of finding you. I'd have turned left if I'd known."

" I don't believe you. You started out with the hope of seeing me, and it's no use pretending anything different."

He led the way up the path and, walking round the corner, they came to a small grey cottage built on the side of the hill. There were some rough buildings at the back, and a strip of land for potatoes. She followed him in, bending her head under the low doorway. The room was small and square. Mary looked around her in disgust.

" Don't you ever do any cleaning? " she asked him. " You ought to be ashamed of yourself. Leave me that bucket of water and find me a brush." She set to work at once. " How long has your mother been dead? "

" Seven years this Christmas," he answered. " Because of my father being hanged and Matt drowned and Joss gone off to America and me growing up wild, she turned religious, and used to pray here by the hour, calling on the Lord. I couldn't bear that, so I ran away to sea. But the sea didn't suit my stomach, and I came back home. I found Mother as thin as a rake. ' You ought to eat more,' I said. But she wouldn't listen to me, so I went off again and stayed in Plymouth for a time, earning a shilling or two in my own way. I came back and found the place empty and the door locked. They told me my mother had died. She'd been buried three weeks. . . . What's the matter? "

" It will be a good thing when there's not a Merlyn left in Cornwall! It's better to have disease in a country than a family like yours. You and your brothers were born twisted and evil. Do you never think of what your mother must have suffered? "

Jem looked at her in surprise.

"Mother was all right. She never complained. She was used to us. . . . How's the landlord of Jamaica Inn?"

"He has had too much to drink, like his father before him."

"That'll be the ruin of Joss," said his brother seriously. "One day he'll kill himself with drink. The fool! Has anything been happening at Jamaica?"

"We had Mr. Bassat from North Hill last week."

"You did? What had the magistrate to say to you?"

"Uncle Joss was away from home. Mr. Bassat was determined to come into the inn and search the rooms. He broke down the door at the end of the passage, but the room was empty. He seemed disappointed, and very surprised, and he rode away in a bad temper. He asked about you, as it happened, and I told him I had never even seen you."

Jem's face was without expression as she told her story, but when she came to the end of her sentence, and the mention of himself, he laughed. "Why did you lie to him?" he asked.

"It seemed less trouble at the time. If I'd thought longer, no doubt I'd have told him the truth. You've got nothing to hide, have you?"

"Nothing much, except that the black horse you saw by the stream belongs to him. He was grey last week, and worth a small fortune to Mr. Bassat. I'll get a few pounds for him at Launceston if I'm lucky. Come down and have a look at him."

They went out into the sun.

"What did Mr. Bassat expect to see at Jamaica Inn?"

Mary looked him straight in the eyes. "You ought to know that better than I do," she answered.

"It was lucky for Joss the stuff had been moved," he said quietly. "It's only a matter of time before they catch him. All he does in self-defence is to drink too much, the fool."

Mary said nothing. If Jem was trying to trap her by seeming honest, he would be disappointed.

"You must have a good view from that little room over

the front door," he said. "Do they wake you from your sleep?"

"How do you know that's my room?" Mary asked quickly.

She saw the surprise in his eyes. Then he laughed. "The window was wide open when I rode into the yard the other morning: I've never seen a window open at Jamaica Inn before."

The excuse was hardly good enough for Mary. A horrible suspicion came into her mind. Could it have been Jem who had hidden in the empty guest room that Saturday night? Something went cold inside her.

"What does it matter to you how much I know? All I think about is getting my aunt away from the place as soon as possible. As for your brother, he can drink himself to death for all I care. His life is his own, and so is his business. It's nothing to do with me."

Jem whistled. "So smuggling doesn't worry you after all? But supposing he were concerned with other things—supposing it were a question of life and death, and perhaps murder—what then?"

"I don't know what you mean," said Mary.

He looked at her for a long time without speaking.

"Perhaps not," he said at last, "but you'll come to know, if you stay long enough. Why does your aunt look so pale? Ask her, next time the wind blows from the north-west. . . . Why are you going? It's early yet; it won't be dark until after four. What's the matter with you?" He took her face in his hands and looked into her eyes. "I believe you're frightened of me. You think I've got barrels of wine and spirits and rolls of tobacco in the little bedrooms above, and that I'm going to show them to you, and then cut your throat. That's it, isn't it? We're a wild lot of fellows, we Merlyns, and Jem is the worst of us all. Is that what you're thinking?"

She smiled back at him in spite of herself. "Something of the sort. But I'm not afraid of you; you needn't think that. I would even like you, if you didn't remind me so much of your brother."

" I can't help my face," he said, " and I'm a much better-looking man than Joss; you must admit that."

" Oh, you've confidence enough to make up for all the other qualities you lack, and I'll not argue about your face. Now let me go."

" Are you coming to Launceston with me on Christmas Eve? "[1]

" What will you be doing over at Launceston, Jem Merlyn? "

" Only selling Mr. Bassat's horse for him, my dear. Say you're coming."

" Supposing you are caught in Launceston with Mr. Bassat's horse? "

" No one's going to catch me. Take a risk, Mary; don't you like excitement? You must be soft, down near Helford."

" All right, Jem Merlyn. You needn't think that I'm afraid. I'd just as soon be in prison as live at Jamaica Inn, anyway. How do we get to Launceston? "

" I'll take you there in the cart, with Mr. Bassat's horse behind us."

Mary was not afraid. To prove it, she would ride beside him in his cart to Launceston on Christmas Eve. She walked away up the hill without a backward look.

Darkness was falling as she crossed the road and went into the yard at Jamaica Inn. The door was opened by her aunt, who seemed pale and anxious.

" Your uncle has been asking for you all day. Where have you been? "

" I was walking on the moors—why should Uncle Joss ask for me? He never has anything to say to me."

" You must speak nicely to him. This is the bad time, when he's getting over it. . . . He'll be bad-tempered—violent perhaps. You mustn't pay any attention to him at times like these. He's not really himself."

The long evening passed, and still there was no call from

[1] *Christmas Eve*—the day before Christmas Day.

the landlord. Mary's eyes closed in spite of herself. In a dream she heard her aunt whisper " I'm going to bed. Your uncle must have settled down for the night." Mary felt sleep come upon her. She dreamed that she was crossing the stream again. Her feet were wet. It was cold . . . much too cold . . . she must climb up the bank. . . . Mary opened her eyes and found that she was lying on the kitchen floor beside the ashes of the fire. The kitchen was cold. The light was low. She trembled, and stretched her stiff arms. Then she saw the door of the kitchen open very slowly, little by little, an inch at a time. Suddenly it was thrown wide open. Joss Merlyn stood there.

At first she thought that he had not seen her; his eyes were fixed on the wall in front of him. She bent low. Slowly he turned in her direction. When his voice came, it was hardly above a whisper. "Who's there? What are you doing? Why don't you speak?" His face was grey. His eyes fastened on her without recognition.

She waited, holding her breath. He moved forward into the room, his head bent, his hands feeling the air, and he crept slowly along the floor towards her. Mary could feel his breath on her face.

" Uncle Joss," she said softly, " Uncle Joss. . . ."

He stayed where he was, looking down at her, and then he leant forward and touched her. "Mary? Is it you, Mary? Why don't you speak to me? Where have they gone? Have you seen them?"

"There's no one here—only myself. Aunt Patience is upstairs. Are you ill? Can I help you?'"

He looked about him, searching the corners of the room.

"They can't frighten me," he whispered. "Dead men can't harm the living. . . . It's dreams; all dreams! The faces stand out like living things in the darkness, and I wake with the sweat pouring down my back. I'm thirsty, Mary; here's the key; go into the bar and fetch me some drink."

When she got back he was sitting at the table, his head in his hands. At first she thought that he was asleep again, but at the sound of her footsteps he lifted his head. She put the bottle and the glass on the table in front of him. He filled the glass.

"You're a good girl. I'm fond of you, Mary. You've got sense, and you've got courage. They ought to have made you a boy." He swallowed the drink, smiling foolishly. Then he pointed his finger. "They pay gold for this. It's the best that money can buy. King George himself hasn't anything better. They can't catch me, Mary; I'm too clever; I've been at the game too long. There are over a hundred of us now, working towards the border from the coast. I've seen blood in my time, Mary, and I've seen men killed dozens of times, but this game beats it all—it's running side by side with death." He seized hold of Mary's arm. "It's that cursed drink that makes a fool of me. I'm as weak as a rat when it has hold of me, you can see that. And I have dreams; I see things that frighten me. I've killed men with my own hands, pushed them under water with my feet, beaten them with rocks and stones; and I've never thought more about it; I've slept in my bed like a child. But when I've had too much to drink I see them in my dreams. I see their white-green faces in front of me, with their eyes eaten by fish; and some of them torn, with the flesh hanging on their bones in ribbons, and some of them have seaweed in their hair. . . ." His face was close to Mary's, his reddened eyes looking into hers, and his breath on her cheek. "Did you never hear of wreckers before?" he whispered. "I've seen men on the ship's ladders and ropes like a mass of flies. They hang on there for safety, shouting in fear at the sight of the breaking waves. Just like flies they are, spread out on the ropes—little black dots of men. I've seen the ship break up beneath them, and the ropes break like thread, and they'll be thrown into the sea, to swim for their lives. But when they reach the shore they're dead men, Mary." He wiped his mouth on the back of his hand; his eyes never left her face. "Dead men tell no stories, Mary." She felt sick, and her hands and her feet were icy-cold. She could see the pale faces of the drowned men, their arms above their heads; she could hear the cries of fear. She trembled again.

She looked at her uncle, and saw that he had slipped forward in his chair, and his head had fallen on his chest. His mouth was wide open, and he breathed noisily as he slept. His arms rested on the table before him, and his hands were folded as if in prayer.

9

ON Christmas Eve the sky was cloudy and threatened rain. Mary leant out of the window, and the soft wet wind blew upon her face. In an hour's time Jem Merlyn would be waiting for her on the moor, to take her to Launceston market. Whether she met him or not depended upon herself, and she could not make up her mind. She had grown older in four days, and the face that looked back at her from her cracked glass was pale and tired. There were dark rings under her eyes. Sleep came to her late at night, and she had no desire for food. For the first time in her life, she saw a likeness between herself and Aunt Patience. If she tightened her mouth and bit her lips, it might be Aunt Patience who stood there, working her mouth, with the straight brown hair framing her face. The habit was an easy one to catch, as was the continuous twisting of her hands. Mary turned away from the glass and began to walk up and down her small room. They shared a secret now, a secret that must never be spoken between them. Mary wondered how many years Aunt Patience had kept that knowledge to herself in silence. In her own way, Aunt Patience was a murderer too. She had killed by her silence.

There remained Jem Merlyn. He broke into her thoughts against her will, and she did not want him. There was enough filling her mind without Jem. He was too like his brother. His eyes, his mouth, and his smile. She knew why Aunt Patience had made a fool of herself ten years ago. It would be easy enough to fall in love with Jem Merlyn. He lacked tenderness; he was rude; he was a thief and a liar. He stood for everything she feared and hated, but she knew she could love him. Jem Merlyn was a man, and she was a woman. She knew she would have to see him again. Today she would go to Launceston with Jem Merlyn, and this time it was he who would answer her questions; he would realise that she was no longer afraid of them, but could destroy them when she chose. And tomorrow—well, tomorrow could take care of itself. There was always Francis Davey and his promise; there would be peace and shelter for her in the house at Altarnun.

This was a strange Christmas time, she thought, as she walked across the East Moor. In the distance she saw a little group coming towards her—the horse, the cart, and two horses led behind. The driver raised his whip in a signal of welcome. Mary felt the colour in her face. He whistled as he drew near, and threw a small package at her feet. " A happy Christmas to you," he said. " I had a silver piece in my pocket yesterday, so I had to spend it. There's a new handkerchief for your head."

She had meant to be silent on meeting him, but this made it difficult. " That's very kind of you," she said, " but I'm afraid you've wasted your money."

" That doesn't worry me. I'm used to it," and he looked at her in that cool way of his. " You were early here. Were you afraid I'd be going without you? "

She climbed into the cart beside him. " Mother and I used to drive into Helford once a week on market days. It all seems very long ago. I have a pain in my heart when I think of it, and how we used to laugh together, even when times were bad. You wouldn't understand that, of course. You've never cared for anything but yourself."

They rode along in silence. Jem was playing with his whip. Mary looked out of the corner of her eye at his hands, and saw that they were long and thin; they had the same strength, the same grace, as his brother's. These attracted her; the others frightened her. She realised for the first time that love and hate ran side by side; that the boundary line was thin between them. The thought was an unpleasant one. Supposing this had been Joss beside her, ten, twenty years ago? She shut the comparison in the back of her mind, fearing it. She knew now why she hated her uncle.

His voice broke in upon her thoughts. " What are you looking at? "

She lifted her eyes. " I happened to notice your hands," she said shortly; " they are like your brother's. . . . How far do we go across the moor? Isn't that the road winding away over there? "

" We join it lower down and miss two or three miles of it. So you notice a man's hands, do you? I should never have believed it of you. You're a woman after all, then, and not a half-grown farm-boy! Are you going to tell me why you have sat in your room for days, or do you want me to guess? Women love to be mysterious."

" There's no mystery in it. You asked me last time we met why my aunt looked as she does. Well, I know now, that's all."

" What are you going to do about it? "

Mary said: " I haven't made up my mind. I have to consider Aunt Patience. You don't expect me to tell you, do you? "

" Why not? I'm not concerned with Joss."

" You're his brother, and that's enough for me."

"Do you think I'd waste my time working for my brother? He can put a rope round his own neck. I may have helped myself to some tobacco now and then, and I've smuggled goods, but I'll tell you one thing, Mary Yellan, and you can believe it or not as you like; I've never killed a man—yet." He cracked the whip fiercely over the horse's head. " So you think I wreck ships, do you, and stand on the shore and watch men drown? And then put my hands into their pockets afterwards, when they're swollen with water? It makes a pretty picture."

Whether his anger was pretended or sincere she could not say, but his mouth was set firmly, and there was a flaming spot of colour high on his cheek.

" You haven't said yet that you don't."

" If you believe it of me, why do you drive with me to Launceston? "

" For the sake of your bright eyes, Jem Merlyn! I ride with you for no other reason," and she met his eyes without hesitation.

He laughed at that, and shook his head, and began whistling again; and all at once there was ease between them, and a certain boyish friendliness. The very boldness of her words had deceived him. He suspected nothing of the weakness that lay behind them, and for the moment they were companions in spite of being man and woman.

They came now to the road, and as the horse increased speed the cart rolled along, with the two stolen horses running behind. It was a happy and rather heated party that reached Launceston that afternoon. Mary had thrown trouble and responsibility to the winds and in spite of her determination in the morning she had given herself to gaiety. Away from the shadow of Jamaica Inn her natural youth and high spirits returned. She laughed because he made her; there was excitement in the air—a sense of Christmas. The streets were filled with people; the little shops were gay. This was a happy world to Mary. She wore the handkerchief that Jem had given her. They had left the horse and cart at the top of the town, and now Jem pushed his way through the crowd, leading his two stolen horses, Mary following close behind him. He led the way with confidence, making straight for the main square. Before long a man pushed through the crowd and came up to the horses. His voice was loud and important. He kept hitting his boot with his whip, and then pointing to the horses. Mary judged him to be a dealer. Soon he was joined by a little sharp-eyed man in a black coat, who now and again touched his arm and whispered in his ear.

Mary saw him look hard at the black horse that had

Mary saw him look hard at the black horse

belonged to Mr. Bassat; he went up to him, and bent down and felt his legs. Then he whispered something in the ear of the loud-voiced man. Mary watched him, feeling afraid.

"Where did you get this horse?" said the dealer, touching Jem on the shoulder. "Never on the moors, not with that head and shoulders."

"I bought him at a year old from old Tim Bray; you remember Tim? He sold his farm last year and went to Dorset. Tim always told me I'd get my money back on this horse. Have a look at him, won't you? But he's not going cheap, I'll tell you that. Look at those shoulders; there's quality for you! I tell you what, I'll take eighteen pounds for him." The sharp-eyed man shook his head but the dealer hesitated.

"Make it fifteen and we might do business," he suggested.

"No, eighteen is my price, and not a penny less."

The two men talked together, and appeared to disagree. At last the dealer nodded. "All right," he said aloud, "I've no doubt you're right. Perhaps we should be wise to have nothing to do with it. You can keep your horse," he added to Jem. "My friend doesn't like him. Take my advice and bring down your price. If you have him for long you'll be sorry." And he pushed his way off through the crowd, with the sharp-eyed man beside him, and they disappeared in the direction of the White Hart Hotel. Mary breathed in relief when she saw them go.

Jem sold the other horse to a cheerful farmer. It began to get dark in the market square, and the lamps were lit. Mary was thinking of going back to the cart when she heard a woman's voice behind her.

"Oh, look James! Did you ever see such a delightful horse in your life? He holds his head just like poor Beauty did. The likeness would be quite striking, only this animal of course is black. What a nuisance Roger isn't here. I can't disturb him in his meeting. What do you think of him, James?"

Her companion said, 'Curse it, Maria, I don't know anything about horses. The horse you lost was grey, wasn't it?

This thing is black, absolutely coal black, my dear. Do you want to buy him? "

" It would be such a good Christmas present for the children. They've been worrying poor Roger ever since Beauty disappeared. Ask the price, James, will you? "

The man came forward. " Here, my good fellow," he called to Jem, " do you want to sell that black horse of yours? What is your price? "

" Twenty-five pounds," said Jem. " I'm not anxious to sell him."

The lady swept towards him. " I'll give you thirty for him. I'm Mrs. Bassat, from North Hill, and I want the horse as a Christmas present for my children. Mr. Bassat is in Launceston now, but I want the horse to be a surprise to him as well. My man shall fetch the horse immediately, and ride him to North Hill before Mr. Bassat leaves the town. Here's the money."

Jem took off his hat and bowed low. " Thank you, madam," he said. " I hope Mr. Bassat will be pleased with your bargain. You will find the horse very safe with children."

" Oh, I'm certain he will be delighted. Of course, the horse is not at all like the one we had stolen. Beauty was a fine horse, and worth a great deal of money. But this little animal is pretty enough, and will please the children. Come along, James; It's getting quite dark."

Jem looked hastily over his shoulder, and touched on the arm a boy who stood behind him. " Here," he said, " would you like a five-shilling piece? " The boy showed that he would, his mouth open in surprise. " Hold on to this horse, then, until the servant comes for him, will you? Here, take him. A happy Christmas to you! "

And he was away in a moment, walking hard across the square, his hands in his pockets. Mary followed, ten yards behind. The laughter rose up inside her, and she hid her mouth in her wrap. She was near to bursting when they got out of sight of the people.

" Jem Merlyn, you deserve to be hanged," she said, when

she could stop laughing. " To stand there in the market square and sell that stolen horse back to Mrs. Bassat herself! The hair on my head has gone grey with watching you."

He threw back his head and laughed, and she could not resist him. Their laughter filled the street. Jem caught her hand. " You're glad you came now, aren't you? "

They threw themselves into the crowded market. Jem bought Mary a bright-red wrap and gold rings for her ears. They sucked oranges beneath a striped tent, and had their future told by an old woman. " Do not trust a dark stranger," she said to Mary, and they looked at each other and laughed again. " There's blood on your hand, young man," she told him. " You'll kill a man one day." " What did I tell you in the cart this morning? " said Jem. " There's no blood on my hands yet. Do you believe me now? " But she shook her head at him and she would not say. Drops of rain fell on their faces, but they did not care. The wind rose.

Jem dragged Mary into the shelter of a doorway, his arms around her shoulders, and he turned her face towards him, and kissed her. " Do not trust a dark stranger," he said, and he laughed, and kissed her again. The night clouds had come up with the rain, and it was dark in an instant.

" You don't want to ride in an open cart in this wind, do you? It's coming from the coast, and we'll be blown over on the high ground. We'll have to spend the night together in Launceston."

" Very likely! Go and get the horse and cart, Jem, while this shower stops for the moment. I'll wait for you here."

" You'll be wet to the skin on the Bodmin road! Pretend you're in love with me, can't you? You'd stay with me then."

" Are you talking to me like this because I'm the barmaid at Jamaica Inn? "

" I like the look of you, and that's enough for any man. It ought to be enough for a woman, too."

" Perhaps it is, for some. I don't happen to be made that way."

" All right, I'll get the horse and cart, and take you home

to your aunt, but I'll kiss you first, whether you like it or not."
He took her face in his hands. "One for sorrow, two for joy!
I'll give you the rest when you are in a more yielding state of
mind."

Then he bent his head against the rain and she saw him
disappear round the corner.

Mary waited, moving her feet and blowing upon her hands.
The long minutes passed, and still he did not come. Mary was
cold and tired. At last she could bear it no longer, and she
set off up the hill in search of him. The long street was empty,
except for one or two people who sheltered in doorways as
she had done. The rain was continuous, and the wind blew
hard. There was nothing left now of the Christmas spirit.

The White Hart Hotel looked welcoming enough, with its
lighted windows, but there was no sign of the horse and cart.
Mary's heart sank. Surely Jem had not started back without
her? She hesitated a moment, and then she went to the door
and passed inside. The hall seemed to be full of gentlemen,
talking and laughing. Her country clothes and wet hair caused
surprise, and a servant came up to her at once and told her to
go. "I've come in search of Mr. Jem Merlyn," said Mary
firmly. "He came here with a horse and cart. I'm sorry to
trouble you, but I'm anxious to find him. Will you please
make some enquiry?"

She turned her back on the little group of men who stood
by the fire and watched her. Among them she recognised the
dealer and the sharp-eyed man.

"If it's the dark fellow who tried to sell my friend a horse
this afternoon, I can tell you about him," said the little man,
showing a row of broken teeth. Laughter came from the group
by the fire.

She looked from one to the other. "What have you to
say?"

"He was in the company of a gentleman only ten minutes
ago," answered the sharp-eyed man, still smiling, and looking at her rudely. "With the help of some of us he was persuaded to enter a carriage that was waiting at the door. He

resisted at first, but a look from the gentleman appeared to decide him. No doubt you know what happened to the black horse? The price he was asking was undoubtedly high."

His remark brought fresh laughter from the fire. Mary looked steadily at the little sharp-eyed man.

" Do you know where he went? "

" No. And I regret to say that your companion left you no parting message. But, it is Christmas Eve. It's not pleasant weather outside. If you like to wait here until your friend returns, myself and these gentlemen will be delighted to entertain you. Come in and rest, and forget him."

Mary turned her back on him and passed out through the door once more. As it closed behind her she heard their laughter.

She stood in the empty market square with the wind and the scattered showers of rain for company. So the worst had happened, and the stolen horse had been recognised. There was no other explanation. Jem had gone. Did they hang men for stealing as well as for murder? She felt ill, and her brain was in confusion. She could make no plans. She supposed that Jem was lost to her now, anyway, and she would never see him again. The adventure was over.

There was no gaiety left in Launceston any more; it was a cold, grey, hateful place. She walked along with the rain beating in her face, knowing little where she went and not caring that eleven miles lay between her and her bedroom at Jamaica Inn. She walked on. Then out of the darkness she saw a carriage coming up the hill. Its progress was slow, with the full force of the wind against it. She watched it with dull eyes. It was passing her, when suddenly she ran after it and called to the driver wrapped up in a coat on the seat. " Are you taking the Bodmin road? Have you a passenger inside? " The driver shook his head and whipped his horse, but before Mary could step aside, " What does Mary Yellan do alone in Launceston on Christmas Eve? " said a voice from inside.

The voice was gentle. A pale face looked out at her from

inside the carriage; white hair and white eyes beneath the broad black hat. It was the vicar of Altarnun.

She watched his face in the darkness; his thin nose curved downward like the beak of a bird, his lips narrow and colourless, pressed firmly together. He leant forward with his chin resting on a walking-stick that he held between his knees. For the moment she could see nothing of his eyes; they were hidden by the short white eyelashes; and then he turned in his seat and looked at her, and the eyes that looked upon her were white also, expressionless as glass.

"So we ride together for the second time," he said, and his voice was soft and low, like the voice of a woman. "Once more I have the good fortune to help you on your way. Well?" He looked steadily at her, and she found herself trying to give an explanation of her day. As before at Altarnun, there was something about him that made her sound like a fool, for she came out of the story badly—just another woman who had made herself cheap at Launceston market and had been left by the man of her choice to find her way home alone.

"What was the name of your companion?" he asked quietly; and she hesitated, awkward and uncomfortable, her sense of guilt stronger than ever.

"He was my uncle's brother."

"You mean the brother knows nothing of the landlord's trade by night?" continued the gentle voice beside her. "He is not of the company who bring the waggons to Jamaica Inn?"

"I don't know," she said. "I have no proof. He admits nothing. But he told me one thing, that he had never killed a man. And I believe him. He also said that my uncle was running straight into the hands of the law, and that they would catch him before long. He surely would not say that if he were one of the company. . . . You told me before that you knew Mr. Bassat. Perhaps you have some influence with him. Could you persuade him to deal mercifully with Jem Merlyn, when the time comes? After all, he is young; he

could start life again. It would be easy enough for a man in
your position."

"I know Mr. Bassat only very slightly," he told her gently.
"Once or twice we have spoken of matters which concern
our two villages. It is hardly likely that he would pardon a
thief because of me, especially if the thief is guilty and happens to be the brother of the landlord of Jamaica Inn. How
old are you?"

"Twenty-three."

"You are very young, Mary Yellan," he said softly; "you
are nothing but a chicken with the broken shell still around
you. Women like you have no need to spill tears over a man
met once or twice; and a first kiss is not a thing to be remembered. You will forget your friend with his stolen horse very
soon. Come, now, dry your eyes; you are not the first to bite
your nails over a lost lover."

He treated her problem lightly. She wondered why he had
not used the words of comfort expected from a priest. She
remembered that last ride with him, when he had whipped
his horse into a fever of speed, and how he had bent forward
in his seat and had whispered under his breath words she had
not understood. Again she felt something of the same dis-
comfort, which she connected with his strange hair and eyes,
as though his unusual appearance cut him off from the rest
of the world.

"So I was right in my guess, and all has been quiet at
Jamaica Inn?" he said after a while.

At once she remembered the full story of the past week,
and the new knowledge that had come to her.

"Mr. Davey," she whispered, "have you ever heard of
wreckers?"

It was too dark in the carriage to see his face, but she heard
him swallow. "My uncle is one of them. He told me so
himself." Still her companion made no reply, and she went
on in a whisper. "They are in it, every one of them, from
the coast to the river bank, all those men I saw that first
Saturday in the bar at the inn—the sailors, the wanderers,

the pedlar with the broken teeth. They've murdered women and children with their own hands; they've held them under water; they've killed them with rocks and stones. Those are death waggons that travel the road by night, and the goods they carry are from wrecked ships, bought at the price of blood. And that's why my uncle is feared and hated by the people in the cottages and farms, and why all doors are barred against him, and why the coaches drive past the inn in a cloud of dust. They suspect what they cannot prove. There, Mr. Davey; now you know the truth about Jamaica Inn."

"So the landlord talks when he has had too much to drink?" he said, and it seemed to Mary that his voice lacked something of its usual gentle quality, but when she looked at him his eyes looking back at her seemed, as usual, cold and without feeling.

"He talks, yes. That's how I know. And perhaps that's why I've lost faith in humanity, in God and in myself; and why I acted like a fool today in Launceston."

The wind had increased in force. The carriage shook. There was no shelter now; the moor on either side was bare, and the clouds flew fast over the land. There was a soft wet feeling in the wind that had come from the sea fifteen miles away.

Francis Davey leant forward in his seat. "We are coming to the turning that leads to Altarnun. The driver is going on to Bodmin and will take you to Jamaica Inn. I shall leave you at the turning and walk down to the village. Am I the only man to know your secret, or do I share it with the land-lord's brother?"

"Jem Merlyn knows," she said. "We spoke of it this morning. He said little, though, and I know that he is not friendly with my uncle. Anyway, it doesn't matter now. Jem is going to prison for another crime."

"And suppose he could save himself by telling about his brother, what then, Mary Yellan? There's a thought for you."

Mary was surprised by this new idea. But the vicar of Altarnun must have read her thoughts. "That would be a relief to you and to him, no doubt, if he had never helped with the wrecking. But there is always the doubt, isn't there? And neither you nor I knows the answer. A guilty man does not usually tie the rope round his own neck."

Mary made a helpless movement with her hands, and he laid his hand on her knee.

"I will tell you one thing to comfort you. A week from now will bring the New Year. The false lights have burnt for the last time, and there will be no more wrecks."

"I don't understand you. How do you know this, and what has the New Year to do with it?"

He called the driver to stop the horse. "I am returning tonight from a meeting in Launceston. Those of us present were informed that at last the Government were prepared to guard the coast. There will be watchers on the cliffs, and the paths now known only to men like your uncle and his companions will be followed by officers of the law. There will be a chain across England, Mary, that will be very hard to break. Now do you understand?" He opened the door of the carriage and stepped out into the road. "Your troubles are over. Tomorrow is Christmas Day, and the bells at Altarnun will be ringing for peace and goodwill. I shall think of you." He waved his hand to the driver, and the carriage went on without him.

There were still three miles to go, and those miles were the wildest of all. She sat in the corner of the carriage. Through the open window, travelling down on the wind, she heard a shot, and a distant shout and a cry. The voices of men came out of the darkness, and the sound of feet upon the road. She leant out of the window. The road rose steeply from the valley, and there in the distance were the tall chimneys of Jamaica Inn. Down the road came a company of men, led by one who carried a light before him as he ran. Another shot sounded, and the driver of the carriage slipped over in his seat and fell. The horse went towards the edge of the road like a blind thing. The carriage swung wildy, then was still. Somebody laughed; there was a whistle and a cry.

A face appeared in the carriage window, a face crowned with wild hair above the reddened eyes. The lips were parted to show white teeth. One hand held a light, the other a smoking gun; they were long, thin hands, things of beauty and grace, though the rounded nails were dirty. Joss Merlyn laughed; then he pulled her out beside him on the road, holding the light above his head so that all could see her. There were ten or twelve of them standing in the road, with torn and dirty clothes, half of them as much the worse for drink as their leader, wild eyes rolling in their bearded faces; one or two had guns in their hands, or were armed with broken bottles, knives and stones. Harry the pedlar stood holding the horse's head, while face-downwards on the road lay the driver of the carriage, his arm bent under him, his body still. When they saw who she was, a shout of laughter broke from the men, and the pedlar put two fingers to his mouth and whistled.

The landlord seized her loose hair in his hand and twisted it like a rope. " So it's you, is it? You've chosen to come back again? "

Mary said nothing. She looked from one to the other of the men in the crowd and they pushed in upon her, laughing, pointing to her wet clothes and shouting insults.

" So you can't talk? " cried her uncle, and hit her across the face with the back of his hand. She put up an arm to protect herself, but he knocked it away and, holding her wrist, he twisted it behind her back. She cried with the pain, and he laughed again.

" I'll tame you, if I kill you first. Do you think you can stand against me, with your monkey face and your boldness . . . and what do you think you are doing at midnight, riding in a hired carriage, with your hair down your back? " He twisted her wrist again, and she fell. " You're nothing but a common——"

" Leave me alone! " she cried; " you have no right to speak to me. You're a murderer and a thief, and the law knows it too. The whole of Cornwall knows it. Your game is over,

Uncle Joss. I've been to Launceston today to give information against you."

A roar came from the group of men; they pressed forward, shouting at her and questioning, but the landlord swore at them, waving them back.

"Get back, you fools! Can't you see she's trying to save herself by lies?" he thundered. "How can she give information about me when she knows nothing? She's never walked the eleven miles to Launceston. Look at her feet. She's been with a man somewhere down the road, and he sent her back on wheels. Get up!" He pulled her to her feet. Then he pointed to the sky, where the low clouds blew before the wind and a star shone. "Look there! There's a break in the sky, and the wind's going east. There'll be more wind still, and a wild grey morning on the coast in six hours' time. We'll waste no more time here. Come on, you lazy devils, don't you want to feel gold and silver run through your hands? Who'll come with me?"

A shout rose from a dozen voices, and hands were raised in the air. One fellow burst into song, waving a bottle over his head. The pedlar pulled at the horse. Joss Merlyn stood for a moment, looking at Mary with a foolish smile, then he pulled her towards the carriage, threw her on the seat in the corner, and then, leaning out of the window, he shouted to the pedlar to whip the horse up the hill. His cry was repeated by the men who ran beside him, and some of them jumped on to the step and held on to the empty driver's seat and hit the horse with sticks. Sweating with fear, he went up the hill at a run, with half a dozen madmen close behind him.

Jamaica Inn was a mass of lights. The doors were open and the windows were wide.

The landlord placed his hand over Mary's mouth and forced her back against the side of the carriage. "You'd give information against me, would you? You'd run to the law, and have me swinging on a rope's end? All right then! You shall stand on the shore, Mary, and you shall watch for the daylight and the coming in of the tide. You know what that means, don't you? You know where I'm going to take you? You think you're not afraid of me, don't you? You scorn me, with your pretty white face and your monkey eyes. Yes—I've had too much to drink! The drink is in charge. Tonight we shall ride for the last time. And you shall come with us Mary—to the coast. . . ."

He turned away from her, shouting to his companions, and the horse, frightened by his cry, started forward again, pulling the carriage behind him, and the lights of Jamaica Inn disappeared into the darkness.

10

IT was a terrible journey of two hours or more to the coast, and Mary, hurt and shaken by her rough treatment, lay in the corner of the carriage, caring little what happened to her. A sudden stillness brought her back to the world, and the cold damp air blowing upon her face through the open carriage window.

She was alone. The men had gone, taking their light with them. The carriage had been stopped in a narrow valley with high banks on either side, and the horse had been taken away. The valley appeared to slope down sharply, the track becoming rough and broken. Mary could see only a few yards. She tried the handle of the door, but it was locked. Then she listened. Carried up towards her on the wind came the sound of the sea. The valley was a way down to the shore. Mary trembled. Somewhere in the darkness below, her uncle and his companions waited for the tide.

Mary considered the size of the window. The door was locked, she knew, but she might force her body through the narrow window-frame. She struggled and pushed, and then she lost her balance, and fell to the ground below.

The drop was nothing, but the fall shook her and she felt

blood run down her side where the window had caught her. She gave herself a moment to rest, and then she dragged herself to her feet and began to move uncertainly up the road, in the dark shelter of the bank. She had not yet formed a plan, but, with her back turned away from the sea, she would be putting distance between herself and the men. This track, winding upwards and to the left, would take her to the high ground of the cliffs.

She found her way along, sometimes kicking a stone, her hair blowing into her eyes. Coming round a sharp corner, she put up her hands to push back the loose curls from her eyes, and because of this she did not see a man kneeling against the bank with his back towards her, his eyes watching the winding track ahead. She came against him, knocking the breath from his body, and he, taken by surprise, fell with her, crying out in fright and anger. They fought on the ground, her hands tearing at his face, but he was too strong for her. He leant on her, breathing heavily, and then he looked closely at her, showing broken yellow teeth. It was Harry the pedlar.

He expected her to cry or struggle but when she did neither, he moved his weight on to his arm and smiled at her in an ugly way. " Didn't expect to see me, did you? Thought I was down on the shore with the landlord and the rest! But now you're here, I'll make you very welcome." He was smiling still. She moved quickly, striking out at him, and she hit him on the point of the jaw. In a second she had struggled from under him and pulled herself to her feet. She searched for a stone to throw at him, but finding nothing but loose earth and sand, she scattered this in his face and eyes, so that he was blinded momentarily. Then she turned again, and began to run like a hunted thing up the twisting track, her mouth open, her hands outstretched, falling over the stones in the path, all sense of direction gone, her one idea to escape from Harry the pedlar.

A wall of cloud closed in on her, blocking out the distant line of bushes at which she had been aiming, and she stopped at once, knowing the danger of low cloud, and how it might deceive her into coming back to the road again. Progress now was slow, but she knew that she was increasing the distance between herself and the pedlar, which was the only thing that mattered. She had no idea of the time; it was three, perhaps four, in the morning, and the darkness would give no sign of breaking for many hours. Once more the rain came down through the curtain of cloud, and it seemed as if she could hear the sea on every side of her and there was no escape from it. The breaking waves, though she could not see them, were somewhere out in the darkness, and to her surprise it seemed that they were on a level with her, not beneath her. This meant that the track must have been only a few yards from the sea itself. The high banks had cut off the sound of the waves. Even as she decided this, there was a gap in the cloud ahead of her. Directly in front of her were the high waves breaking upon the shore.

After a time, when her eyes had accustomed themselves to the shadows, she saw, grouped against a large rock on the beach, a little knot of men, silently looking ahead of them into the darkness. Their stillness made them more threatening. She waited. They did not move.

The cloud began to lift very slowly, showing the outline of the coast. To the right, in the distance, where the highest part of the cliff sloped to the sea, Mary could just see a light. At first she thought it was a star. But the star was a false light placed there by her uncle and his companions. They waited, all of them, standing on the stones with the waves breaking beyond their feet. Mary watched with them. Then out of the cloud and darkness came another light in answer to the first. And now Mary could see the shadowed outline of a ship and the white sea boiling around it. Closer drew the ship's light to the light upon the cliff, like a flying thing coming to a flame.

Mary could bear no more. She got to her feet and ran out over the sand, shouting and crying, waving her hands above her head, lifting her voice to fight against the sea and the wind, which threw it back to her in scorn. Someone caught

. . . the shadowed outline of a ship

hold of her and forced her down on to the stones. She was stepped upon and kicked. Her cries died away as a rough cloth covered her mouth; her arms were dragged behind her and tied together, the rope cutting into her flesh.

They left her then, with the waves sweeping towards her not twenty yards away, and as she lay there helpless, she heard the cry that had been hers become the cry of others, and fill the air with sound. The cry rose above the noise of the sea, and was seized and carried by the wind; and with the cry came the terrible sound of splitting, breaking wood and the thunder of the waves. Mary saw the great black mass that had been the ship roll slowly on its side. Clinging to it were little black dots that fell one by one into the white sea.

A terrible sickness came upon Mary and she closed her eyes, her face pressed to the stones. The men who had waited during the cold hours waited no more. They ran like madmen backwards and forwards on the sand, shouting. They walked waist-deep in the waves, careless of danger, seizing the goods carried in on the tide. They were animals, fighting and tearing things from one another. One of them lit a fire in the corner by the cliff, the flames burning strongly and fiercely in spite of the rain. The treasure from the sea was dragged over the sand and heaped beside it. The fire cast a yellow light upon the scene and threw long shadows over the sand where the men ran backwards and forwards.

When the first body was washed on to the shore they gathered round it, diving among the remains with searching hands, picking it as clean as a bone. There was no system in their work tonight. They robbed here and there, mad with the success they had not planned—dogs at the heels of their master whose idea had proved so splendid. They followed him where he ran amongst the breaking waves, the water streaming from him; he was larger and stronger than them all.

The tide turned, and a new coldness came upon the air. A grey colour came upon the water and was answered by the sky. At first the men did not notice the change. And then

Joss Merlyn himself lifted his great head; he shouted suddenly, calling the men to silence, pointing to the sky that was pale now. They hesitated, looking once more at the things which rose and fell in the sea; and then they all turned and began to run towards the entrance to the little valley, silent once more, their faces grey and frightened in the growing light. Success had made them careless. The day had broken upon them; the world was waking up; night, that had been their friend covered them no more.

It was Joss Merlyn who tore the cloth away from her mouth and pulled Mary to her feet. He threw her over his shoulder and ran over the stones to the entrance to the valley; and his companions, caught up already in fear, threw some of the goods they had seized from the sea upon the backs of the horses tied up there. Their movements were hurried. The carriage, stuck in the bank half-way up the valley, resisted their efforts to pull it out. Some of them began to scatter up the road. Here on the coast, where every face was known, strangers would be noticed; but a wanderer could make his way alone, finding his own path. These running men were cursed by those who remained, struggling with the carriage, and now, through stupidity and haste, it was pulled from the bank in so rough a manner that it overturned, rolling upon one side and breaking a wheel.

There was a wild rush to the remaining farm-cart that had been left farther up the road, and to the already overloaded horses. Someone, still obedient to the leader, put fire to the broken carriage, whose presence in the road meant danger to them all. A terrible fight broke out between man and man for possession of the farm-cart that might yet carry them away to safety. Those who carried guns now had the advantage, and the landlord, with his remaining supporter Harry the pedlar by his side, stood with his back to the cart and shot into the crowd. This won the cart for the landlord. The remaining men, frightened by the sight of their dying fellows, turned all at the same moment and scattered up the twisting lane, anxious only to put a safe distance between themselves and their former leader. The landlord leant against the cart with the smoking, murderous gun, blood running freely from a cut on his eye. Now that they were alone, he and the pedlar wasted little time. The goods that had been brought up the valley they threw on the cart beside Mary. The main store was still down on the sand and washed by the tide. They dared not risk collecting it; there was not a moment to spare. The two men who had been shot lay in the road beside the cart. Their bodies bore witness, and must be destroyed. It was Harry the pedlar who dragged them to the fire. It was burning well; much of the carriage had disappeared already, while one red wheel stuck up above the blackened and broken wood.

Joss Merlyn led the remaining horses to the cart, and without a word the two men climbed in and whipped them into action. Lying on her back in the cart, Mary watched the low clouds pass across the sky. Darkness had gone; the morning was damp and grey. From far away across the fields came the merry sound of church bells. She remembered suddenly that it was Christmas Day.

11

THE square of glass was familiar to her. It was larger than the carriage window, and there was a crack across it that she remembered well. She kept her eyes on it, struggling with memory, and she wondered why she no longer felt the rain on her face and the steady current of wind. Mary cried, and turned her head restlessly from side to side; out of the corner of her eye she saw the brown, discoloured wall beside her, and the rusty nail-head where a picture had once hung.

She was lying in her bedroom at Jamaica Inn.

Now there was a face bending down to her, and she drew back, her hands in front of her, because the ugly mouth and broken teeth of the pedlar were still in her mind. Her hands

were held gently, though, and the eyes that looked at her,
reddened like her own from crying, were watery and blue.

It was Aunt Patience.

"How long have I lain here?" Mary questioned, and she
was told that this was the second day. She sat up in bed
and swung her legs to the floor, her head aching with the
effort.

"What are you going to do?" Aunt Patience pulled at
her, but her niece shook her aside and began to drag on
her clothes.

"Aunt Patience, I have gone through enough out of loyalty
to you. You can't expect me to bear any more. Whatever
Uncle Joss may have been to you once, he is not human now.
He's a beast, half mad with drink and blood. Men were murdered by him on the coast; don't you understand? Men were
drowned in the sea. I can see nothing else. I shall think of
nothing else until my dying day."

The door opened; the landlord of Jamaica Inn stood outside the room. He looked lined and grey; the cut above his
eye was still bright red. He was dirty and unwashed, and
there were black shadows under his eyes.

"I thought I heard voices in the yard, but I saw no one.
Did you hear anything?" Nobody answered. He sat down on
the bed, his hands picking at the bedclothes, his eyes wandering from the window to the door.

"He'll come. He's sure to come. I've made sure of my own
death; I've disobeyed him. He warned me once, and I laughed
at him; I didn't listen. I wanted to play the game on my own.
It means death for us, for all three of us sitting here. We're
finished, I tell you; the game is up. Why did you let me
drink? Why didn't you break every bottle in the house, and
turn the key on me? I'd not have hurt you. Now it's too late;
the end has come."

He looked from one to the other of them, his reddened
eyes hollow; the women looked back without understanding.

"What do you mean?" said Mary at last. "Who are you
afraid of? Who warned you?"

He shook his head, and his hands wandered to his mouth, the fingers restless. "No," he said slowly, "my secrets are still my own. But I tell you one thing—and you're in it now as much as Patience there—we have enemies on either side of us now. We have the law on one hand, and on the other . . ." He stopped himself, the old look in his eyes once more. "You'd like to know, wouldn't you? You'd like to run out of the house with the name on your lips. You'd like to see me hanged. All right, I don't blame you for it. Let's get out of here. This room smells of damp and decay."

They followed him without a word. He led the way to the kitchen, where the door was locked and the window barred. Wooden shutters[1] were closed over the window. Then he turned and faced the women.

"We've got to think out a plan. We've been sitting here for nearly two days now, like rats in a trap. And I've had enough, I tell you. I never could play that sort of game."

His wife crept over to him and touched his sleeve, passing her tongue over her lips.

"Well, what is it?" he said fiercely.

"Why can't we creep away now, before it's too late? We'd be in Launceston and then out of the county in a few hours. We could travel by night. We could aim for the eastern counties."

"You fool!" he shouted. "Don't you realise that there are people on the road between here and Launceston who think I'm the devil himself—who are only waiting their chance to accuse me of every crime in Cornwall? The whole county knows by now what happened on the coast on Christmas Eve, and if they see us running away they'll have the proof. Don't you think I've wanted to get away and save myself? No, we've got one chance—one single chance in a million. We've got to lie quiet. If we stay here at Jamaica they may start scratching their heads. They've got to look for proof. They've got to get sworn proof before they lay hands on us. Oh, yes,

[1] *shutters*—hinged wooden "doors" that can be closed to protect a window.

the ship's there with her back broken on the rocks, and piles of stuff lying on the sand ready to take away—put there by someone, they'll say. They'll find two bodies burnt right up, and a heap of ashes. Many of us will be suspected, but where's the proof? Answer me that. *I* spent Christmas Eve here with my family! "

" You've forgotten one thing, haven't you? " said Mary.

" No, my dear, I have not. The driver of that carriage was shot not quarter of a mile down the road outside. You were hoping we'd left the body there, weren't you? The body travelled with us to the coast and it lies now, if I remember rightly, beneath a ten-foot bank of sand. Of course, someone is going to miss him; I'm prepared for that; but as they'll never find his carriage it does not matter much. Perhaps he was tired of his wife and has driven to Penzance. They can look for him there."

He threw back his head and laughed; but his laugh broke off short in the middle, his mouth shut like a trap, his face as white as a sheet. " Listen," he whispered, " listen. . . ."

They followed the direction of his eye fastened upon the crack of light that came through the narrow gap in the shutters. Something was scraping gently at the kitchen window . . . tapping lightly, softly, scratching at the glass. There was no other sound in the kitchen except the frightened breathing of Aunt Patience, whose hand crept along the table to her niece. Mary watched the landlord as he stood motionless on the kitchen floor. Then he bent forward until his fingers fastened themselves upon his gun that stood against the chair, never once taking his eyes from the gap in the shutters. He sprang forward, swinging the shutters open. A man stood outside the window, his face pressed against the glass, his broken teeth showing in a twisted smile. It was Harry the pedlar. Joss Merlyn swore, and threw open the window. " Come inside, can't you? Do you want to be shot, you fool? Unfasten the door, Mary." She opened the door without a word. " Well, have you brought news? " questioned the land-lord.

The pedlar pointed over his shoulder. " The country's wild with anger; they're mad for blood and justice. There'll only be one end to this storm, Joss, and you know the name for it, don't you? " He made a sign with his hands across his throat. " We've got to run," he said. " It's our only chance. The roads are poison, and Bodmin and Launceston worst of all. I'll keep to the moors; it'll take me longer, I know that, but what's that matter if you save yourself from hanging? "

" So you'll give up Harry, will you? Run like a beaten dog? Have they proved it on us? Tell me that. Or has your conscience gone against you? "

" Curse my conscience, Joss; it's common sense I'm thinking of. This part of the country is dangerous, and I'll go from it while I can. I've stayed by you, haven't I? I've come out here today, risking death, to give you warning. I'm not saying anything against you, Joss, but it was your stupidity that brought us to this, wasn't it? You made us mad like yourself, and led us to the coast on an adventure that none of us had planned. We took a chance in a million—and succeeded. Too well. We became stupid with excitement, left a hundred tracks scattered on the sand. And whose fault was it? Why, yours, I say! " He banged the table, his yellow face pushed close to the landlord's.

Joss Merlyn considered him for a moment, and when he spoke his voice was dangerous and low. " So you accuse me, do you, Harry? You're like the rest of your kind when the luck of the game turns against you. Run, then, if you like; run to the river bank like a beaten dog. I'll fight the world alone! "

The pedlar forced a laugh. " We can talk, can't we, without cutting each other's throats? I've not gone against you; I'm on your side still. We were all mad on Christmas Eve, I know that; let's leave it alone, then; what's done is done. Our men are scattered, and we needn't worry about them. They'll be too frightened to show their heads. That leaves you and me, Joss. We've been in this business, the pair of us, deeper than most, and the more we help each other, the better it'll be for us both. Now then, that's why I'm here, to talk and see what we ought to do."

The landlord watched him calmly. "Just what are you aiming at, Harry?" he said, filling his pipe.

"I'm not aiming at anything. I want to make things easier for all of us. We've got to go, unless we want to hang. But it's like this, Joss; I don't see the fun of going empty-handed. There's a lot of stuff we put in the store-room two days ago. That's right, isn't it? It belongs to all of us who worked for it on Christmas Eve. But there's none of them left to claim it except you and me. I'm not saying that there's much of value there, but I don't see why some of it shouldn't help us out of the county, do you?"

The landlord blew a cloud of smoke into his face. "So you didn't come back to Jamaica Inn because of my sweet smile alone, then? I was thinking you were fond of me, and wanted to hold my hand."

The pedlar smiled, and changed his position on his chair. "All right—we're friends, aren't we? There's no harm in plain speaking. The stuff's here, and it'll take two men to move it. The women can't do it. What's against you and I making a bargain?"

The landlord thoughtfully smoked his pipe. "And supposing the stuff isn't here, after all? Supposing I've got rid of it already? I've been sitting here for two days, you know, and the coaches pass my door. What then, Harry boy?"

The smile faded from the face of the pedlar. "What's the joke? Do you play a double game up here at Jamaica Inn? You'll find it hasn't paid you, if you have. You've been clever at this trade, month in, month out; too clever some of us thought, for the small profit we made out of it, who took most of the risks. And we didn't ask you how you did it. Listen here, Joss Merlyn; do you take your orders from someone above you?"

The landlord was on him like a flash. He hit him on the point of the jaw, and the man went over backwards on to his head. He recovered instantly, and got to his knees, but the landlord towered above him, his gun pointing at the pedlar's throat.

"Move, and you're a dead man," he said softly.

Harry the pedlar looked up at his attacker, his little eyes half closed.

"Now we can talk, you and I." He leant once more against the table, while the pedlar knelt on the floor. "You didn't come here tonight to warn me; you came to see what you could get out of the wreck. You didn't expect to find me here, did you? You thought it would be Patience here, or Mary; and you would frighten them easily, wouldn't you, and reach for my gun where it hangs on the wall, as you've often seen? You little rat, Harry, do you think I didn't see it in your eye when I threw back the shutters and saw your face at the window? Do you think I didn't see your surprise? Very well, then. We'll make a bargain, as you suggest. I've changed my mind, my loving friend, and with your help we'll take the road. There's stuff in this place worth taking, nor can I load alone. Tomorrow is Sunday, and a day of rest. Not even the wrecking of fifty ships will drag the people from their knees. There'll be prayers offered for poor sailors who suffer because of the devil's work, but they'll not go looking for the devil on Sunday.

"Twenty-four hours we have, Harry my boy, and tomorrow night when you've broken your back loading my property into the farm-cart and kissed me good-bye—why, then you can go down on your knees and thank Joss Merlyn for letting you go free with your life."

He raised his gun again, bringing it close to the man's throat. The man cried out, showing the whites of his eyes. The landlord laughed.

"Come on," he said, 'do you think I'm going to play with you all night? Open the kitchen door, and turn to the right, and walk down the passage until I tell you to stop. Your hands have been waiting to explore the goods brought from the shore, haven't they, Harry? You shall spend the night in the store-room among it all." Putting his gun in the pedlar's back, he pushed him out of the kitchen and down the dark passage to the store. The door had been mended with new wood and was stronger than before.

After he had turned the key on his friend, the landlord returned to the kitchen .

"I thought Harry would turn soon," he said. "I've seen it coming in his eyes for weeks. He'll fight on the winning side, but he'll turn against you when your luck changes. He's jealous of me. They're all jealous of me. They knew I had brains, and they hated me for it. You'd better get your supper and go to bed. You have a long journey to make tomorrow night, and I warn you here and now it won't be an easy one."

Mary looked at him across the table. Tired as she was, because all that she had seen and done weighed heavily on her, her mind was full of plans. Some time, somehow, before tomorrow night, she must go to Altarnun. Once there, her responsibility was over. Action would be taken by others. It would be hard for Aunt Patience, hard for herself at first, perhaps, but at least justice would win. It would be easy enough to clear her own name, and her aunt's. The thought of her uncle standing as he would with his hands bound behind him, powerless for the first time and for ever, was something that gave her great pleasure. She dragged her eyes away from him. "I'll have no supper tonight," she said.

He crossed into the hall as she climbed the stairs, and he followed her to the room over the front door. "Give me your key," he said, and she handed it to him without a word. He stayed for a moment, looking down at her, and then he bent low and laid his fingers on her mouth.

"I've a liking for you, Mary. You've got spirit still, and courage, for all the rough treatment I've given you. I've seen it in your eyes tonight. If I'd been a younger man I'd have fallen in love with you—and won you too, and ridden away with you. You know that, don't you? " He lowered his voice to a whisper. "There's danger for me ahead. Never mind the law. The whole of Cornwall can come running at my heels

and I shall not care. It's other things I have to watch for—
footsteps, Mary, that come in the night and go again, and a
hand that would strike me down. We'll put the river between
us and Jamaica Inn," he said; and then he smiled, the curve
of his mouth painfully familiar to her and known like something from the past. He shut the door upon her, and turned
the key.

She went then to her bed. And she began to cry, softly and
secretly, the tears tasting bitter as they fell upon her hand.

12

SHE had fallen asleep where she lay, without undressing,
and her first conscious thought was that the storm had
come again. She was awake at once, and she waited for the
sound that had woken her to come again. It came in an
instant, a shower of earth thrown against the window from
the yard outside.

It was Jem Merlyn standing below in the yard. He whispered up to her, "Come down to the door here, and unfasten
it for me."

She shook her head. "I cannot do that. I am locked here
in my room." He looked back at her, puzzled, and he
examined the house as if it might offer some solution of its
own. He ran his hand along the wall, feeling for rusty nails
that might have been used for training climbing plants long
ago, and might give him a foothold of a sort. Swinging himself to the low roof over the front door, he was able to push
his body against the wall of the house and in this manner to
pull himself up to the level of her window.

"I shall have to talk to you here," he said. "Come closer
where I can see you." She knelt on the floor of her room, her
face at the window, and they looked at each other without
speaking. He looked tired, and his eyes were hollow like those

of one who has not slept. There were lines about his mouth that she had not noticed before, and he did not smile.

"I owe you an apology," he said at last. "I left you alone without excuse at Launceston on Christmas Eve. You can forgive me or not, as you feel. But the reason for it—that I can't give you. I'm sorry."

She was hurt by his manner. His coolness damped her flame, and she drew back inside herself at once. He did not even ask how she returned that night. "Why are you locked in your room?" he questioned.

Her voice was flat and dull when she replied. "My uncle fears that I may wander in the passage and discover his secrets."

"Where is my brother?"

"He is going to spend the night in the kitchen. He is afraid of something, or someone; the windows and doors are barred, and he has his gun."

Jem laughed bitterly. "I don't doubt he is afraid. He'll be more frightened still before many hours have passed, I can tell you that. I came here to see him, but if he sits there with a gun across his knee I can postpone my visit until tomorrow, when the shadows have gone."

"Tomorrow may be too late."

"What do you mean?"

"He intends to leave Jamaica Inn tonight."

"Are you telling me the truth?"

"Why should I lie to you now?"

Jem was silent. The news had clearly come as a surprise to him. She was thrown back now upon her old suspicion of him. He was the visitor expected by her uncle, and therefore hated by him and feared. The face of the pedlar returned to her, and his words, that had stung Joss Merlyn to anger: "Listen here, Joss Merlyn, do you take your orders from someone above you?" The man whose brains made use of the landlord's strength, the man who had hidden in the empty room. . . .

Leaning forward suddenly, he looked into her face and

touched the long scratch on one side. "Who did this?" he said, turning from the scratch to the mark on the jaw. She hesitated a moment, and then answered him.

"I got them on Christmas Eve."

The look in his eye told her at once that he understood, and had knowledge of the evening, and because of it was here now at Jamaica Inn.

"You were with them, on the shore?" he whispered. "Why did you go with them?"

"They were mad with drink. I don't think they knew what they were doing. I could no more have stood against them than a child. There were a dozen of them or more, and my uncle . . . he led them. He and the pedlar. If you know about it, why do you ask me? Don't make me remember. I don't want to remember."

"How much did they hurt you?"

"Marks, scratches—you can see for yourself. I tried to escape and I hurt my side. They caught me again, of course. They bound my hands and feet, and tied a cloth over my mouth so that I could not cry out. I saw the ship come through the darkness, and I could do nothing—alone there in the wind and the rain. I had to watch them die."

She broke off, her voice trembling, her face in her hands. He made no move towards her; and she felt him far from her, wrapped in secrecy.

"Was it my brother who hurt you most?" he said after a while.

It was too late; it did not matter now. "I've told you he had had too much to drink. You know, better than I perhaps, what he can do then."

"Yes, I know." He paused for a moment, and then he took her hand. "He shall die for this."

"His death will not bring back the men he has killed."

"I'm not thinking of them now."

"If you're thinking of me, don't waste your sympathy. I can revenge myself in my own way. I've learnt one thing at least—to depend upon myself."

"What do you intend to do?"

"He expects me to go with him, and Aunt Patience as well. If I asked you to do something, how would you answer me?"

He smiled then, for the first time, as he had done in Launceston, and her heart warmed at once, encouraged at the change.

"How can I tell?" he said.

"I want you to go away from here."

"I'm going now."

"No, I mean away from the moors—away from Jamaica Inn. I want you to tell me you won't return here. I can stand up against your brother; I'm in no danger from him now. I don't want you to come here tomorrow. Please promise me you'll go away."

"What have you got in your mind?"

"Something which does not concern you, but might bring you to danger. I can't say any more. I would rather you trusted me."

"Trust you? Of course I trust you. It's you who won't trust me, you little fool." He laughed silently, and bent down to her, putting his arms round her, and kissed her then as he had kissed her in Launceston, but with anger.

"Play your own game by yourself, then, and leave me to play mine. If you must be a boy, I can't stop you, but for the sake of your face, which I have kissed, and shall kiss again, keep away from danger. You don't want to kill yourself, do you? I have to leave you now; it will be day in less than an hour. And if both our plans go wrong, what then? Would you mind if you never saw me again? No, of course you would not care. You'll marry a farmer one day, or a small tradesman, and live quietly among your neighbours. Don't tell them you once lived at Jamaica Inn, or had love made to you by a horse-thief. They'd shut their doors against you. Good-bye—and good fortune to you."

He lowered himself to the ground. She watched him from the window, waving to him, but he had turned and gone without looking back at her, crossing the yard like a shadow. Morning would soon be here; she would not sleep again.

She sat on her bed, waiting until her door should be unlocked; and she made her plans for the evening to come. She must act as if she were prepared to make the proposed journey with the landlord and Aunt Patience. Then, later, she would make some excuse—a desire to rest in her room before the journey, perhaps—and then would come the most dangerous moment of her day. She would have to leave Jamaica Inn secretly and run to Altarnun. Francis Davey would understand; time would be against them, and he must act quickly. She would then return to the inn, and hope that her absence had remained unnoticed. That was the risk. If the landlord went to her room and found her gone, her life would be worth nothing. She must be prepared for that. No excuse would save her then. But if he believed her to be sleeping still, the game would continue. They would make preparations for the journey; they might even climb into the cart and come out upon the road. After that, her responsibility would end. Their fate would be in the hands of the vicar of Altarnun. Beyond this she could not think, nor had she any great desire to look ahead.

When she had helped them clear the midday meal away and had persuaded her aunt of the necessity of packing a basket of food for the journey, she turned to her uncle and spoke to him.

" If we are to travel tonight, would it not be better if Aunt Patience and myself rested now during the afternoon, and so could start out fresh upon the journey? There will be no sleep for any of us tonight."

" You may rest if you like. There'll be work for both of you later. You are right when you say there will be no sleep for you tonight. Go, then; I shall be glad to get rid of you for a time."

Mary entered her own little room and closed the door, turning the key. Her heart beat fast at the thought of adventure. It was nearly four miles to Altarnun by road, but she could walk the distance in an hour. If she left Jamaica at four o'clock, when the light was failing, she would be back again soon after six; and the landlord would be unlikely to come to wake her up before seven. She had three hours, then, in which to play her part. She would climb out of the window and drop to the ground, as Jem had done. She sat by the window, looking out upon the bare yard and the high road where no one ever passed, waiting for the clock in the hall to strike four.

When it struck at last, the sound rang out in the silence. Every second was precious to her now, and she must waste no time in going. She climbed through the window. The jump was nothing, as she had thought. She looked up at Jamaica Inn. It looked evil in the approaching darkness, the windows barred; she thought of the terrible things the house had witnessed, the secrets now shut up behind its walls; and she turned away from it as from a house of the dead, and went out upon the road.

Darkness fell as she walked. She came at last to where the roads branched, and she turned to her left, down the steep hill to Altarnun.

The vicar's house was silent. There were no lights there. She turned back towards the church. Francis Davey would be there, of course! It was Sunday. She hesitated a moment, uncertain what to do. Then the gate opened and a woman came out into the road, carrying flowers.

She looked hard at Mary, knowing her to be a stranger, and would have passed her by with a good night, but Mary turned. " Forgive me," she said. " I see you have come from the church. Can you tell me if Mr. Davey is there? "

" No, he is not," said the woman; and then, after a moment, " Were you wishing to see him? "

" Very urgently," said Mary. " Can you help me? "

The woman looked at her curiously, and then shook her head.

" I am sorry," she said. " The vicar is away. He went away

She climbed through the window

to preach in another village, many miles from here. He is not expected back in Altarnun tonight."

13

AT first Mary looked back at the woman without believing her. "But that is impossible. Surely you are mistaken?"

"The vicar has left. He rode away after dinner. I ought to know; I keep house for him."

Mary wondered in despair what she could do now. To come to Altarnun and then return without help to Jamaica Inn was impossible. She could not place confidence in the village people, nor would they believe her story. She must find someone with power—someone who knew something of Joss Merlyn and Jamaica Inn.

"Who is the nearest magistrate?' she said at last.

The woman considered the question. "Why, the nearest would be Mr. Bassat over at North Hill, and that must be over four miles from here—perhaps more, perhaps less. I cannot say for certain, for I have never been there. You would surely not walk out there tonight?"

"I must. There is nothing else for me to do. I must waste no time, either. I am in great trouble now, and only your vicar or a magistrate can help me."

"You'd better stay here and wait for the vicar, if you can."

"That is impossible," said Mary, "but when he does return, could you tell him perhaps that . . . But wait; if you have pen and paper I will write him a note of explanation. That would be better still."

"Come in to my cottage here, and you may write what you like. I can take the note to his house."

Mary followed the woman to the cottage. The time was slipping away fast. Her uncle would take warning from the fact that she had run away, and leave the inn before the intended time. And then her effort would have been in vain. . . .

Mary wrote with the haste of despair. Then she folded the note and gave it to the woman by her side. So she set out on a walk of four miles or more to North Hill.

She had placed such faith in Francis Davey that it was hard to realise that he had failed her. He had not known, of course, that she needed him. She was anxious about Aunt Patience, and the thought of her setting out upon the journey like a trembling dog tied to its master made Mary run along the bare white road. She came at last to big gates and the entrance to a private road. This must be North Hill, and this house must belong to the magistrate. Away in the distance a church clock struck seven. She had been away for about three hours already from Jamaica Inn. Her fear returned as she came to the house. She swung the great bell and waited. After some time she heard footsteps inside, and the door was opened by a manservant. " I have come to see Mr. Bassat on very urgent business," she told him. " The matter is of the greatest importance, otherwise I would not disturb him at such an hour, and on a Sunday night."

" Mr. Bassat left for Launceston this morning," answered the man. " He was called away hurriedly, and he has not yet returned."

This time Mary could not control herself, and a cry of despair escaped her.

" I have come some way," she said, with great feeling, as if by her very despair she could bring the magistrate to her side. " If I do not see him, something terrible will happen, and a great criminal will escape the hands of the law. You look at me curiously, but I am speaking the truth. If only there were someone I could turn to. . . ."

" Mrs. Bassat is at home," said the man, stung with curiosity. " Perhaps she will see you, if your business is as urgent as you say. Follow me, will you, to the library? "

Mary crossed the hall in a dream, knowing only that her

plan had failed again, through chance alone, and that she was now powerless to help herself. The wide library, with its bright fire, seemed unreal to her, and her eyes were unaccustomed to the light that met them. A woman whom she recognised immediately as the lady who had bought the horse in Launceston market square was sitting in a chair in front of the fire. She looked up in surprise when Mary was shown into the room.

Mrs. Bassat rose to her feet at once. "What can I do for you?" she said kindly. "You look pale and tired. Won't you sit down?"

Mary shook her head impatiently. "Thank you, but I must know when Mr. Bassat is returning home."

"I have no idea," replied his lady. "He had to leave this morning at a moment's notice, and, to, tell you the truth, I am really anxious about him. If this innkeeper decides to fight, as he is certain to do, Mr. Bassat may be wounded, in spite of the soldiers."

"What do you mean?" said Mary quickly.

"Why, he has set out on a highly dangerous piece of work. Your face is new to me, and I suppose you are not from North Hill, otherwise you would have heard of the man Merlyn who keeps an inn upon the Bodmin road. Mr. Bassat has suspected him for some time of terrible crimes, but it was not until this morning that the full proof came into his hands. He left at once for Launceston to get help, and he intends to surround the inn tonight, and seize the people inside. He will go well armed, of course, and with a large body of men, but I shall not rest until he returns."

"I came here to warn Mr. Bassat that the landlord intended to leave the inn tonight, and so escape justice. I have proof of his guilt, which I did not believe Mr. Bassat to possess. You tell me that he has already gone, and perhaps even now is at Jamaica Inn. Therefore I have wasted my time in coming here."

Mary sat down then, her hands folded, and looked unseeing into the fire. She had come to the end of her strength and for the moment she could not look ahead. All that her tired mind could tell her was that her journey this evening had been in vain.

"I have done a very senseless thing in coming here," she said hopelessly. "I thought it clever, but I have only succeeded in making a fool of myself and of everyone else. My uncle will discover that my room is empty, and guess at once that I have given information against him. He will leave Jamaica Inn before Mr. Bassat arrives."

Mrs. Bassat came towards her. "You have been placed in a fearful position," she said kindly, "and I think you are very brave to come here tonight, all those lonely miles, to warn my husband. The question is: what do you want me to do now? I am willing to help you in any way you think best."

"I can think of nothing but my poor aunt, who at this moment may be suffering terribly. I must know what is happening at Jamaica Inn, if I have to walk back there myself tonight."

"But you cannot possibly walk back there now, alone. I will order the trap,[1] and Richards shall go with you. He can be trusted completely, and can be armed in case of need. If there is fighting in progress, you need not go near the inn until it is over."

In a quarter of an hour the trap drove up to the door, with Richards in charge. Mary recognised him at once as the servant who had ridden originally with Mr. Bassat to Jamaica Inn. He was burning with curiosity, of course, but she gave short answers to his questions, and did not encourage him. Rapidly the horse and trap covered the miles that Mary had walked alone.

"We shall find them there before us, as likely as not," Richards told Mary. "It will be a good thing for the neighbourhood when he's arrested. It's a pity we were not here sooner; there'll have been some excitement in taking him, I expect."

"Little excitement if Mr. Bassat finds his man has escaped,"

[1] *trap*—light horse-drawn carriage with two wheels.

said Mary quietly. " Joss Merlyn knows these moors like the back of his hand."

" My master was born here, just as the landlord was," said Richards; " if it comes to a run across country, I'd expect my master to win every time. He's hunted here, as man and boy, for nearly fifty years. But they'll catch him before he starts to run, if I'm not mistaken."

The steep hill to Jamaica rose in front of them, white beneath the moon, and as the dark chimneys rose into view, Richards became silent, examining the pistols[1] in his belt. As they drew near to the top of the hill, Richards turned, and whispered in her ear, " Would it be best for you to wait here, in the trap, by the side of the road, and I go forward to see if they are there? "

" I've waited long enough tonight, and gone half mad with it," said Mary. " I'd rather meet my uncle face to face than stay behind here, seeing and hearing nothing. It's my aunt I'm thinking of. She's as harmless as a child, and I want to take care of her if I can. Give me a pistol and let me go. I'll not take any risks, I promise you."

She went forward, then held her pistol in front of her and looked round the corner of the stone wall into the yard. It was empty. The stable door was shut. The inn was as dark and silent as when she had left it nearly seven hours before; the windows and the door were barred. There were no wheel-marks in the yard, and no preparations for escape. She crept across to the stable and laid her ear against the door. She waited a moment, and then she heard the horse move rest-lessly; she heard his feet on the stone floor.

Then they had not gone, and her uncle was still at Jamaica Inn!

Her heart sank, and she wondered if she should return to Richards and wait until the magistrate and his men arrived. Surely, if her uncle intended to leave, he would have gone before now? He might have changed his plans and decided to go on foot, but then Aunt Patience could never go with him.

[1] *pistol*—short gun used with one hand.

Mary went round the corner of the house. She came to where a crack of light would show through a gap in the kitchen window shutter. There was no light. She laid her hand on the handle of the door. It turned, to her astonishment, and the door opened. This easy entrance, entirely unexpected, surprised her for the moment and she was afraid to enter. Supposing her uncle sat on his chair, waiting for her, his gun across his knee? She had her own pistol, but it gave her no confidence.

Very slowly she put her face to the gap made by the door. No sound came to her. Out of the corner of her eye she could see the ashes of the fire, but they were hardly red. She knew then that the kitchen had been empty for hours. She pushed the door open, and went inside. She lit the lamp and looked about her.

The door to the passage was wide open, and the silence became more frightening than before, strangely and terribly still. Something was not as it had been; some sound was lacking that must account for the silence. Then Mary realised that she could not hear the clock. It had stopped. She stepped into the passage and listened again. She was right; the house was silent because the clock had stopped.

She turned the corner, and she saw that the clock, which always stood against the wall beside the door, had fallen forward on to its face. The glass was broken in pieces on the stone floor, and the wood was split. The clock had fallen across the narrow hall, and it was not until she came to the foot of the stairs that Mary saw what was beyond.

The landlord of Jamaica Inn lay on his face among the broken pieces.

The fallen clock had hidden him at first; he lay in the shadow, one arm thrown high above his head and the other fastened upon the door. There was blood on the stone floor; and blood between his shoulders, dark now and nearly dry, where the knife had found him.

When he was attacked from behind he must have stretched out his hands, and fallen, dragging at the clock; and when he fell upon his face the clock had crashed with him to the ground, and he had died there, trying to open the door.

14

IT was a long time before Mary moved away from the stairs. Something of her own strength had gone, leaving her powerless like the figure on the floor. It was the silence that frightened her most. Now that the clock was no longer going, her ears missed the sound of it. Her light shone upon the walls, but it did not reach to the top of the stairs, where the darkness waited for her. She knew that she could never climb those stairs again, nor walk along that upper passage. Whatever lay above her must rest there undisturbed.

She backed away down the hall along the passage, and when she came to the kitchen and saw the door still open, her self-control left her, and she ran blindly through the door to the cold air outside, where the familiar figure of Richards met her. He put out his hands to save her, and she seized him, feeling for comfort, cold now from the shock.

"He's dead," she said; "he's dead there on the floor. I saw him"; and, although she tried hard, she could not stop the trembling of her body. He led her to the side of the road, back to the trap, and he reached for her wrap and put it round her, and she held it closely round her, grateful for its warmth.

"Has your aunt gone?" whispered the man.

Mary shook her head. "I don't know. I did not see. I had to come away."

He saw by her face that her strength had gone. "All right, then," he said, "all right. Sit quiet, then. No one shall hurt you. There now." His rough voice helped her, and she sat close beside him, the warm wrap up to her mouth.

"That was no sight for a girl to see; you should have let

me go. I wish now you'd stayed back here in the trap. That's terrible for you, to see him lying there, murdered."

Talking helped her. "The horse was still in the stable. I listened at the door and heard it moving about. They had never even finished their preparations for going. The kitchen door was not locked, and there were bundles on the floor there, ready to load into the cart. It must have happened several hours ago."

"It puzzles me what the magistrate is doing," said Richards. "He should have been here before this. You should tell your story to him. There's been bad work here tonight."

They fell silent, and both of them watched the road.

"Who'd have killed the landlord?" said Richards puzzled. "He's a match for most men, and should have been able to defend himself. There were plenty who might have been concerned in it, in spite of that. If ever a man was hated, he was."

"There was the pedlar," said Mary slowly. "I'd forgotten the pedlar. It must have been him, breaking out from the barred room."

She fastened upon the idea, to escape from another; and she re-told the story, eagerly now, of how the pedlar had come to the inn the night before. It seemed at once that the crime was proved, and there could be no other explanation.

"He'll not run far before the magistrate catches him," said Richards. "No one can hide on these moors, unless he's a local man, and I have never heard of Harry the pedlar before. But then, they came from every hole and corner in Cornwall, Joss Merlyn's men. They were, as you might say, the rubbish of the county."

He paused, and then: "I'll go to the inn, if you would like me to, and see for myself whether he has left any tracks behind him. There might be something. . . ."

Mary seized hold of his arm. "I don't want to be alone again," she said quickly. "Think me a coward if you will, but I could not bear it. If you had been inside Jamaica Inn tonight you would understand. . . . Something has happened to my aunt as well. I know that. I know she is dead. That's why I was afraid to go upstairs. She is lying there in the darkness, in the passage above. Whoever killed my uncle will have killed her too."

The servant coughed. "She may have run out on to the moor. She may have run for help along the road. . . ."

"No," whispered Mary, "she would never have done that. She would be with him now, by his side. She is dead. I know she is dead. If I had not left her, this would never have happened."

The man was silent. He could not help her. After all, she was a stranger to him, and what had happened was no concern of his.

Mary held up a warning hand. "Listen," she said, "can you hear something?"

They looked to the north. The distant sound of horses was unmistakable. "It's them!" said Richards excitedly. "It's the magistrate; he's coming at last."

They waited. The noise drew near, and Richards in his relief ran out upon the road to greet them, shouting and waving his arms. The leader pulled up his horse, calling out in surprise at the sight of him. "What are you doing here?" he shouted. It was Mr. Bassat himself. He held up his hand to warn his followers behind.

"The landlord is dead, murdered!" cried his servant. "I have his niece here with me in the trap. It was Mrs. Bassat who sent me out here, sir." He held the horse for his master, answering as well as he could the rapid questions put to him.

"If the fellow has been murdered, he deserved it, but I'd rather have put him in chains myself for all that. You cannot punish a dead man."

The magistrate, whose mind worked slowly, did not realise what Mary was doing in the trap. He had thought that she was his servant's prisoner. "This is too difficult for me to understand," he said. "I believed you to be working with your uncle against the law. Why did you lie to me, when I came earlier in the month? You told me you knew nothing."

" I lied because of my aunt," said Mary. "Whatever I said to you then was for her sake only, nor did I know as much then as I do now."

" You did a brave thing in walking all that way to Altarnun to warn me; but all this trouble could have been avoided, and the terrible crime of Christmas Eve could have been prevented if you had been open with me before. But we can talk about that later. I must ask you to wait in the yard."

He led his men round the back, and before long the dark and silent house seemed to come to life. The windows were flung open, and some of the men went upstairs and explored the rooms above. Someone called sharply from the house. After a time the magistrate himself came out into the yard and crossed to the trap.

" I'm sorry," he said. " I have bad news for you. Perhaps you expected it."

" Yes," said Mary.

" I don't think she suffered at all. She was lying just inside the bedroom at the end of the passage. Killed with a knife, like your uncle. She could have known nothing. Believe me, I am very sorry. I wish I could have kept this from you." He stood by her awkwardly; and then, seeing that Mary was better left alone, he walked back across the yard to the inn. Mary sat motionless, and she prayed in her own way that Aunt Patience would understand what she had tried to do, and would forgive her, and find peace now, wherever she might be.

Once again, there was excitement in the house—shouting and the sound of running feet. There was a crash of splitting wood and the shutters were torn away from the windows of the barred room, which no one, it seemed, had entered until now.

Then round the corner of the yard they came, six or seven of them led by the magistrate, holding amongst them something that fought to escape. " They've got him! It's the murderer! " shouted Richards. The prisoner looked up at her, his clothes dirty, his face unshaved and black; it was Harry the pedlar.

"What do you know of this fellow?" the magistrate said to Mary. "We found him in the barred room there lying on the floor. He says he knows nothing of the crime."

"He was one of the company," said Mary slowly, "and he came to the inn last night and quarrelled with my uncle. My uncle aimed a gun at him, and locked him up in the barred room, threatening him with death. He had every reason to kill my uncle, and no one could have done it except he. He is lying to you."

"But the door was locked upon him; it took three of us to break it down from the outside. This fellow had never been out of the room at all. Look at his clothes; look at his eyes, blinded still by our light! He's not your murderer."

Mary knew at once that what Mr. Bassat had said was the truth. Harry the pedlar could not have done the murders.

"We'll have him in prison, in spite of that, and hang him too, if he deserves it, which I'll swear he does. But first he shall give us the names of his companions. One of them has killed the landlord for revenge, you may be sure of that, and we'll track him down if we set every hound[1] in Cornwall on his heels."

They dragged the pedlar away, although he began begging for mercy and swearing, turning his rat's eyes now and again on Mary, who sat above him in the trap a few yards away.

She neither heard his curses nor saw his ugly narrow eyes. She remembered other eyes that had looked at her in the morning, and another voice that had spoken calm and cold, saying of his brother: "He shall die for this." There was the sentence, thrown out carelessly on the way to Launceston fair: "I have never killed a man—yet"; and there was the old woman in the market square: "There's blood on your hands; you'll kill a man one day." All the little things she wanted to forget rose up and shouted against Jem: his hatred of his brother, his cruelty, his lack of tenderness, his bad Merlyn blood. He was one of a kind. He had gone to Jamaica Inn as he had promised, and his brother had died, as he had

---

[1] *hound*—large hunting dog.

"Stop!" he called. *"In the name of the King."*

sworn. The whole truth was before her in its ugliness. He was a thief, and like a thief in the night he had come and gone again. When morning came he would be gone, throwing his legs across a horse, and so away out of Cornwall for ever, a murderer like his father before him.

In her imagination she heard the sound of his horse upon the road, far distant in the quiet night. But the sound she heard was not the dream thing of her imagination, but the real sound of a horse upon the highway. She turned her head and listened. The sound of a horse drew nearer still. She was not alone now as she listened. The men looked towards the road, and Richards went quickly to the inn to call the magistrate. The sound of the horseman was loud now as he came over the top of the hill, and when he came into view Mr. Bassat came out of the inn.

"Stop!" he called. "In the name of the King. I must ask your business on the road tonight."

The horseman turned into the yard. When he bowed and took off his hat, the thick crown of hair shone white under the moon, and the voice that spoke in answer was gentle and sweet.

"Mr. Bassat of North Hill, I believe," he said, and he leant forward in his saddle, with a note in his hand. "I have a message here from Mary Yellan of Jamaica Inn, who asks for my help in trouble; but I see by the company gathered here that I came too late. You remember me, of course; we have met before—I am the vicar of Altarnun."

15

MARY sat alone in the living-room in the vicar's house and looked into the fire. She had slept for a long time, and was now rested and refreshed, but the peace which she desired had not yet come to her. They had all been kind to

her, and patient. The vicar had driven her himself in the trap
to Altarnun, and they arrived there as his church clock struck
one. He called his housekeeper from her cottage near by, the
same woman that Mary had spoken with in the afternoon.
She lit a fire and warmed a rough woollen nightdress before
it, while Mary took off her clothes, and when the bed was
ready for her and the bedclothes turned back, Mary allowed
herself to be led to it like a child.

She would have closed her eyes at once but an arm came
suddenly round her shoulders and a voice said in her ear:
"Drink this." Francis Davey himself stood beside the bed,
with a glass in his hand, his strange eyes looking into hers,
pale and expressionless. "You will sleep now," he said, and
she knew from the bitter taste that he had put some powder
in the hot drink which he had made for her. The last thing
she remembered was those still white eyes that told her to
forget; and then she slept, as he had told her.

It was nearly four in the afternoon before she woke. When
she was dressed, and had gone below to the living-room, to
find the fire burning and the curtains drawn and the vicar out
on some business, it seemed to her that responsibility for the
murders was hers alone. Jem's face was always with her as
she had seen it last, tired and lined in the grey light, and there
had been a determination in his eyes then that she had tried
not to see. He had played an unknown part from beginning
to end, and she had shut her eyes to the truth. She was a
woman, and for no reason in heaven or earth she loved
him. He had kissed her, and she was bound to him for ever.
She felt herself weakened in mind and body, who had been
strong before; and her pride had gone with her independence.

One word to the vicar when he returned, and a message to
the magistrate, and Aunt Patience would be revenged. Jem
would die with a rope round his neck as his father had done,
and she would return to Helford, trying to begin again her
old life. But she knew that the word would never be given.
Jem was safe from her, and he could ride away with a song
on his lips and a laugh at her expense, forgetful of her, and

of his brother, and of God; while she dragged through the years, silent and bitter, coming in the end to be laughed at as a woman who had been kissed once in her life and could not forget it.

She heard the vicar's footsteps on the path outside, and rose hurriedly.

"Forgive me," he said. "You did not expect me so soon." He took out his watch. "You have had supper with me before, Mary Yellan, and you shall have supper with me again; but this time, if you do not mind, you shall prepare the table and fetch the tray from the kitchen. I have some writing to do; that is, if you have no objection."

When the church clock said quarter to seven they sat down together at the table and he helped her to some cold meat.

"I understand from Richards, servant to Mr. Bassat, that you suspected the pedlar of the murder, and said so to Mr. Bassat himself. It is a pity for all of us that the barred room proves that he did not do it. He would have done very well as a man to hang, and saved a lot of trouble."

The vicar ate an excellent supper, but Mary was only playing with her food.

"What has the pedlar done, that you hate him?"

"He attacked me once."

"I thought so. You resisted him, of course?"

"I believe I hurt him. He did not touch me again."

"No, I do not suppose he did. When did this happen?"

"On Christmas Eve."

"After I left you in the carriage?"

"Yes."

"I am beginning to understand. You did not return, then, to the inn that night. You met the landlord and his friends upon the road?"

"Yes."

"And they took you with them to the shore to add to their sport?"

"Please, Mr. Davey, do not ask me any more. I would

rather not speak of that night ever again. There are some things that are best buried deep."

"You shall not speak of it, Mary Yellan. I blame myself for having allowed you to continue your journey alone. . . . When I consider the pedlar, I feel it was very careless of the murderer not to have looked into the barred room. He would most certainly have made the whole affair more thorough."

"You mean, he might have killed him too?"

"Exactly. The pedlar is no ornament to the world. What is more, if the murderer had known that he had attacked you, he would have had a strong enough reason to kill the pedlar twice over."

Mary cut herself a piece of cake which she did not want, and forced it between her lips. But the hand shook that held the knife.

"I don't see," she said, "how I am concerned in the matter."

"You have too modest an opinion of yourself."

They continued to eat in silence, Mary with lowered head and eyes fixed upon her plate. She knew that he was watching her to see the effect of his words. But at last she could wait no longer, but must burst out with a question: "So Mr. Bassat and the rest of you have made little progress after all, and the murderer is still free?"

"The organisation appears to have been far larger than was formerly supposed. In fact, the pedlar even suggested that the landlord of Jamaica Inn was their leader in name only, and that your uncle had orders from someone above him. That of course makes things look very different. What have you to say about the pedlar's idea?"

"It is possible, of course."

"I believe that you once made the same suggestion to me?"

"I may have done. I forget."

"If this is so, it would seem that the unknown leader and the murderer must be the same person. Don't you agree?"

"Why, yes, I suppose so."

"That should make the search easier. We may forget most of the company, and look for someone with a brain and some character. Did you ever see such a person at Jamaica Inn?"

"No, never."

"He must have moved about secretly, possibly in the silence of the night when you and your aunt were asleep. He would not have come by the road, because you would have heard the noise of his horse. So the man must know the moors. That is why Mr. Bassat intends to question every local man within ten miles. So you see the net will close round the murderer, and if he stays long he will be caught. We are all sure of that. Have you finished already? You have eaten very little."

"I am not hungry."

"I am sorry for that. Did I tell you that I saw a friend of yours today?"

"No, you did not. I have no friends but yourself."

"Thank you, Mary Yellan. That is a kind thing to say to me. But you are not being strictly truthful, you know. You have a friend; you told me so yourself."

"I don't know who you mean, Mr. Davey."

"Come, now. Did not the landlord's brother take you to Launceston fair?"

Under the table, Mary dug her finger-nails into her flesh.

"The landlord's brother?" she repeated in order to delay her answer. "I have not seen him since then. I believed him to be away."

"No, he has been in the district since Christmas. He told me so himself. As a matter of fact, it had come to his ears that I had given you shelter, and he came up to me with a message for you. 'Tell her how sorry I am.' That is what he said. I imagine that he meant that he was sorry about your aunt. It was just before I came away from North Hill this evening when the discussion had ended for the day."

"Why was Jem Merlyn present at this discussion?"

"He had a right, I suppose, as brother of the dead man. He did not appear much moved by his death, but perhaps they did not agree."

"Did—did Mr. Bassat and the gentlemen question him?"

"There was a great deal of talk amongst them the whole day. Young Merlyn appears to have brains. His answers were very clever. He must have far better brains than his brother ever had. You told me he lived rather riskily, I remember. He stole horses, I believe."

Mary agreed. Her fingers followed a pattern on the table-cloth.

"He seems to have done that when there was nothing better to do, but when a chance came for him to use his brains, he took it, and one cannot blame him, I suppose. No doubt he was well paid."

The gentle voice wore away at her, and she knew that he had defeated her. She could no longer keep up the pretence that she did not care.

"What will they do to him, Mr. Davey? What will they do to him?"

The pale, expressionless eyes looked back at her, and for the first time she saw a shadow pass across them and a momentary surprise.

"Do?" he said, clearly puzzled. "Why should they do anything? I suppose he has made his peace with Mr. Bassat and has nothing more to fear. They will hardly try to punish him for old crimes after the service he has done them."

"I don't understand you. What service has he done?"

"Your mind works slowly tonight, Mary Yellan. Did you not know that it was Jem Merlyn who gave information against his brother?"

She looked at him stupidly, her brain refusing to work. She repeated the words after him like a child who learns a lesson. "Jem Merlyn gave information against his brother?"

The vicar pushed away his plate, and began to put the supper things on the tray. "Why, certainly. It appears that it was Mr. Bassat himself who took away your friend from Launceston on Christmas Eve, and carried him off to North Hill, as an experiment. 'You've stolen my horse,' he said, 'and you're as big a criminal as your brother. I've the power to throw you into prison tomorrow, and you wouldn't set eyes on a horse for a dozen years or more. But you can go free if you bring me proof that your brother at Jamaica Inn is the man I believe him to be.'

"Your young friend said 'No! You must catch him yourself if you want him.' But the magistrate pushed a big notice under his nose. 'Look here, Jem,' he said, 'and see what you think of that. There's been the bloodiest wreck on Christmas Eve since the *Lady of Gloucester* went on the rocks last winter. Now will you change your mind?' I understand that your friend escaped from his chains and ran away in the night; but he came back again yesterday morning, when they did not expect to see him again, and went straight up to the magistrate and said, as calmly as you please, 'Very well, Mr. Bassat, you shall have your proof.' And that is why I remarked to you just now that Jem Merlyn has a better brain than his brother had."

Mary looked blindly before her into space, her whole mind split, as it were, by his information, the case she had built in such fear and pain against the man she loved falling into nothing like a house of cards.

"Mr. Davey," she said slowly, "I believe I am the biggest fool that ever came out of Cornwall."

"I believe you are, Mary Yellan," said the vicar.

After the gentle voice she knew, his dry words were a punishment in themselves, but she accepted them humbly.

The anxiety and fear had gone from her at last.

"What else did Jem Merlyn say and do?" she asked.

The vicar looked at his watch. "I wish I had time to tell you," he said, "but it is nearly eight already. The hours go by too fast for both of us. I think we have talked enough about Jem Merlyn for the present."

"Tell me something—was he at North Hill when you left?"

"He was. In fact, it was his last remark that hurried me home."

"What did he say to you?"

"He was not speaking to me. He told Mr. Bassat he in-

tended to ride over tonight to visit the blacksmith[1] at Warleggan. It's a long way from North Hill, but I expect he can
find his way in the dark."

" What has it to do with you if he visits the blacksmith? "

" He will show him the nail he picked up in the grass down
in the field below Jamaica Inn. The nail comes from a horse's
shoe; the work was carelessly done, of course. The nail was
a new one, and Jem Merlyn, being a stealer of horses, knows
the work of every blacksmith on the moors. ' Look here,' he
said to the magistrate. ' I found it this morning in the field
behind the inn. I'll ride to Warleggan with your permission, and
throw this in Tom Jory's face as an example of bad work.' "

" Well, and what then? "

" Yesterday was Sunday, was it not? And on Sunday no
blacksmith works unless he has a special respect for the person who needs his help. Only one traveller passed Tom Jory's
workshop yesterday, and begged a new nail for his horse's
shoe, and the time was, I suppose, somewhere near seven
o'clock in the evening. After which, the traveller continued
his journey—a journey which included a visit to Jamaica Inn."

" How do you know this? " said Mary.

" Because the traveller was the vicar of Altarnun," he said.

16

A SILENCE had fallen upon the room. Although the
fire burnt as steadily as ever, the air was cold as it had
not been before. Each waited for the other to speak, and
Mary heard Francis Davey swallow once. At last she looked
into his face, and saw what she expected : the pale, steady eyes
looking at her across the table, cold no longer, but burning in his
white face like living things. She knew now what he wanted her

---

[1] *blacksmith*—man who works with iron, and uses special nails to fasten
shoes to horses.

to know, but still she said nothing, trying to win delay.

" There is no longer any need for pretence between us," he said. " You say to yourself, ' What sort of man is this vicar of Altarnun? ' You say, ' This man is a strange product of nature, and his world is not my world.' You are right there, Mary Yellan. I live in the past—long ago in the beginning of time, when the rivers and the sea were one, and the old gods walked the hills."

He rose from his chair and stood before the fire, a thin black figure with white hair and eyes, and his voice was gentle now, as she had known it first.

" If you studied history you would understand," he said, " but you are a woman, living in the nineteenth century, and because of this my language is strange to you. Yes, I am a strange product of nature and of time. I do not belong here, and I was born with a desire for revenge against our times and against mankind. Peace is very hard to find in the nineteenth century. The silence has gone, even on the hills. I hoped to find it in the Christian church, but its teaching is false. However, we can talk of these things later, when the hunt is not after us. One thing at least, we have no baggage, but can travel light, as they travelled in the old days."

Mary looked up at him, holding tight to the sides of her chair.

" I don't understand you, Mr. Davey."

" Why yes, you understand me very well. You know by now that I killed the landlord of Jamaica Inn, and his wife too; nor would the pedlar have lived if I had known of his existence. You have put the story together in your own mind, while I talked to you just now. You know that it was I who directed every move made by your uncle, and that he was a leader in name alone. He was powerless without my orders, but the greater his fame among his companions the better he was pleased. We were successful, and he served me well; no other man knew the secret of our partnership.

" You were the difficulty, Mary Yellan. When you came among us, I knew that the end was near. In any case we had played the game to its limit and the time had come to make an end. How you troubled me with your courage and your conscience, and how I admired you for it! Of course you had to hear me in the empty bedroom at the inn, and had to creep down to the kitchen and see the rope upon the beam; that was your first piece of interference.

"And then you go out upon the moor after your uncle, who had an appointment with me on Roughtor, and, losing him in the darkness, meet myself and tell me your secrets. Well, I became your friend, did I not, and gave you good advice? Which, believe me, could not have been improved upon by the magistrate himself. Your uncle knew nothing of our strange friendship. He caused his own death, by disobedience. I knew something of your determination, and that time alone would quieten your suspicions. But your uncle had to drink himself to madness on Christmas Eve and, behaving like a fool, put the whole country in a fever. I knew then that when the rope was round his neck he would play his last card and name me as the leader. Therefore he had to die, Mary Yellan, and your aunt, who was his shadow; and, if you had been at Jamaica Inn last night when I passed by, you too—No, you would not have died."

He leant down to her and, taking her two hands, he pulled her to her feet, so that she stood level with him, looking into his eyes.

"No," he repeated, "you would not have died. You would have come with me as you will come tonight."

She looked back at him, watching his eyes. They told her nothing—they were clear and cold as they had been before—but his hold on her wrists was firm, and held no promise of escape.

"You are wrong," she said. "You would have killed me then as you will kill me now. I am not coming with you, Mr. Davey."

"You have proved yourself a dangerous enemy, and I prefer to have you by my side. In time, we will be able to return to our first friendship."

"Any friendship we have have shared was a disgrace and a dishonour. You wear the clothes of a priest of God to shield you from suspicion. You talk to me of friendship. . . ."

"Your refusal and disgust please me more than anything, Mary Yellan," he replied. "There is a fire about you that the women of the old days possessed. Your companionship is not a thing to be thrown aside. Are you ready? Your wrap hangs in the hall, and I am waiting. You understand me, the house is empty, and your cries would be heard by no one. I am stronger than you might suppose. Your uncle knew my strength! I don't want to hurt you, Mary Yellan, but I shall have to do that if you resist me. Come, where is that spirit of adventure that you have made your own? Where is your courage?"

She saw by the clock that he must already have used up his allowance of time. It was half past eight, and by now Jem would have spoken with the blacksmith at Warleggan. Twelve miles lay between them perhaps, but no more. She thought rapidly, balancing the chances of failure and success. If she went now with Francis Davey she would slow down his speed. The law would follow close behind him, and her presence would show where he was in the end. If she refused to go, why then there would be a knife in her heart, at best.

She smiled then, and looked into his eyes, having made her decision.

"I'll come with you, Mr. Davey," she said, "but you will regret it in the end."

"I'll like you the better for it. I'll teach you to live, Mary Yellan, as men and women have not lived for four thousand years or more."

"You'll find me no companion on your road, Mr. Davey."

"Roads? Who spoke of roads? We go by the moors and the hills, and put our feet on granite and grass as the ancient men did before us."

She passed into the passage. She was filled with the wild spirit of adventure, and she had no fear of him, and no fear of the night. Nothing mattered now, because the man she loved was free and had no stain of blood upon him. She could love him without shame; she knew that he would come to her again. In fancy she heard him ride upon the road after them, and she heard his victorious cry.

She followed Francis Davey to where the horses were saddled. This was a sight for which she was not prepared.

"Do you not mean to take the trap?" she said.

"No, Mary, we must travel light and free. You can ride; every woman born on a farm can ride; and I shall lead you."

The night was dark, with damp in the air and a cold wind. The sky was filled with low cloud, and the moon was hidden. There would be no light upon the way, and the horses would travel unseen. The night itself favoured the vicar of Altarnun. She climbed into the saddle, wondering whether a shout and a wild cry for help would wake the sleeping village, but even as the thought passed through her mind she saw the flash of steel in his hand, and he smiled.

"That would be a fool's trick, Mary," he said, "they go to bed early in Altarnun, and by the time they were awake and rubbing their eyes I should be away over the moor and you— you would be lying on your face in the long wet grass and your youth and beauty spoilt. Come now!"

She said nothing. She had gone too far in her game of chance, and must play it to the finish. He put himself on the other horse, fastened hers to it, and they set out on their extraordinary journey.

They came to the edge of the moor and the rough track leading to the stream, and then across the stream and beyond to the great black heart of the moor, where there were no tracks and no paths. The tors rose up around them and hid the world behind, and the two horses were lost between the steep hills. Mary's hopes began to fail, as she looked over her shoulder at the black hills that rose behind her. There was an ancient mystery about these moors. Francis Davey knew their secret, and he cut through the darkness like a blind man in his home.

"Where are we going?" she said, at last, and he turned to her, smiling beneath his wide black hat, and pointed to the north.

"The Atlantic has been my friend before. A ship shall carry us from Cornwall. You shall see Spain, Mary, and Africa, and learn something of the sun; you shall feel the sand under your feet, if you wish. I care little where we go; you shall make the choice. Why do you smile and shake your head?"

"I smile because everything you say is wild and impossible. You know as well as I do that I shall run from you at the first chance—at the first village perhaps. I came with you tonight because you would have killed me otherwise, but in daylight, within sight and sound of men and women, you will be as powerless as I am now."

"I am prepared for the risk. You forget that the north coast of Cornwall is very unlike the south. This north coast is as lonely as the moors themselves, and never a man's face shall you look upon but mine until we come to the harbour that I mean to reach."

"Supposing then that the sea is reached, and we are upon your ship, with the coast behind us. Name any country you please—Africa, or Spain. Do you think that I should follow you there and not tell about you, a murderer of men?"

"You will have forgotten it by then, Mary Yellan."

"Forgotten that you killed my mother's sister?"

"Yes, and more besides. Forgotten the moors, and Jamaica Inn and your own foolish feet that crossed my path. Forgotten your tears on the road from Launceston, and the young man who caused them. . . . Oh, don't bite your lip and look angry. I can guess your thoughts. I have heard confessions in my day, and I know the dreams of women better than you do yourself."

They rode on in silence, and after a time it seemed to Mary that the darkness of the night became thicker and the air closer, nor could she see the hills around her as she had before. The horses picked their way delicately, and now and again stopped as though uncertain of their way. The ground was soft now and dangerous, and though Mary could no longer see the land on either side, she knew by the feel of the soft ground that they were surrounded by marshes. This explained the horses' fear, and she looked at her companion to discover his feelings. He leant forward in his saddle, looking into the darkness that every moment became thicker, and she saw by his thin mouth tight-closed like a trap that he was using all his powers to find their way, threatened suddenly with this new danger. Mary thought of these same marshes as she had seen them in the light of day—the long brown grasses swaying in the wind, while beneath them the black water waited in silence. She knew how the people of the moors themselves could go wrong, so that he who walked with confidence one moment could hesitate the next, and sink without warning. Francis Davey knew the moors, but even he might lose his way.

She heard her companion swallow, and the little trick sharpened her fear. He looked to right and left, and already the damp shone in his hair and on his clothes. Mary smelt the sour smell of rotting plants. And then, in front of them, barring their further progress, there rolled out of the night a great bank of low cloud, a white wall that blocked out every scent and sound.

Francis Davey stopped the horses; they stood trembling, the steam from their sides rising and mixing with the cloud. Then Francis Davey turned to Mary, with the damp on his eyelashes and his hair, and his white face as expressionless as ever.

" The gods have gone against me after all," he said. " To continue now among the marshes would be worse madness than to return. We must wait for the day."

She said nothing, her first hopes returning to her, but then she remembered that the weather would be an enemy to hunters as well as to the hunted.

He urged the horses to the left, away from the low ground, until instead of the yielding grass there was firmer ground and loose stones, while the white cloud moved up with them step by step.

"There will be rest for you, after all, Mary Yellan," he said, "and a cave for your shelter and granite for your bed. Tomorrow may bring the world to you again, but tonight you shall sleep on Roughtor." The horses climbed slowly out of the cloud to the black hills beyond.

Later, Mary sat with her wrap round her, her back against a huge stone. The great tor lifted its broken top like a crown, while below them the clouds hung unchanged. Up here the air was pure and clean. There was a wind that whispered in the stones; its breath, sharp as a knife and cold, blew upon the rocks and sounded in the caves.

The horses were restless; they stood against a rock for shelter, and turned now and again towards their master. He sat apart, a few yards distant from his companion, and sometimes she felt his eyes upon her. This was his kingdom here, alone in the silence, with the great rocks of granite to shield him and the cloud below to hide him. She thought how far they were from normal life. Here on the tor the wind whispered of fear, bringing old memories of violence and despair, and there was a wild, lost note that sounded in the granite high above Mary's head, on the very top of Roughtor, as if the gods themselves stood there with their great heads lifted to the sky. In her fancy she could hear the whisper of a thousand voices and the marching of a thousand feet, and she could see the stones turning into men beside her. Their faces were inhuman, older than time, rough like the granite; and they spoke in a language that she could not understand, and their hands and feet were curved like the feet of a bird. They turned their stone eyes upon her, and looked through her and beyond, paying no attention, and she knew that she was like a leaf in the wind, while they lived on, undying creatures of ancient times. They came towards her, shoulder to shoulder, neither seeing nor hearing her, but moving like blind things to destroy her. . . .

She woke from this dream to reality, feeling the vicar's

hand upon her mouth. She would have struggled with him, but he held her fast, speaking fiercely in her ear and telling her to be still. He forced her hands behind her back and bound them, using his own belt.

Then he took a handkerchief from the pocket of his coat and folded it, and placed it in her mouth, knotting it behind her head so that speech or cry was now impossible. When he had done this he helped her to her feet, and he led her a little way beyond the granite rocks to the slope of the hill. "I have to do this, Mary, for the sake of both of us," he said. "When we set out last night I did not expect this cloud. Listen to this, and you will understand why I have bound you, and why your silence may save us yet."

He pointed downwards to the white cloud below. "Listen," he said again.

The darkness had broken above their heads and morning had come. To the east a faint light came before the pale, unwilling sun. The cloud was with them still, and hid the moors below like a white sheet. Then she listened, as he had told her, and far away, from beneath the cloud, there came a sound between a cry and a call. It was too faint at first to distinguish; it was unlike a human voice, unlike the shouting of men. It came nearer, and Francis Davey turned to Mary, the damp still white on his eyelashes and hair.

"Do you know what it is?" he said.

She looked back at him, and shook her head. She had never heard the sound before.

"I had forgotten that Mr. Bassat keeps hounds in his stables. It is a pity for both of us that I did not remember."

She understood; and with sudden fear of that distant eager crying she looked up at her companion, and from him to the two horses standing patiently as ever by the side of the rock.

"Yes," he said, following her eyes, "we must let them loose and drive them down to the moors below. They would only bring the hounds upon us."

She watched him, sick at heart, as he untied the horses and led them to the steep slope of the hill. Then he bent down to the ground, gathering stones in his hands, and rained blow after blow upon their sides; they ran off in fear, kicking stones and earth on their way, and so disappeared into the white clouds below. The crying of the hounds came nearer now, deep and continuous, and Francis Davey ran to Mary, pulling off his long black coat and throwing his hat away on to the grass.

"Come," he said. "Friend or enemy, we are both in danger now."

They climbed up the hill among the stones and granite rocks, he with his arm round her, because her bound hands made progress difficult; and they ran in and out of pools, struggled knee-deep in wet grass, climbing higher and higher to the top of Roughtor. Here, on the very top, the granite was strangely shaped, one great rock making a sort of roof. Mary lay beneath this great stone, breathless, and bleeding from scratches. He reached down to her, and though she shook her head and made signs that she could climb no farther, he bent and dragged her to her feet again, cutting at the belt that bound her and tearing the handkerchief from her mouth.

"Save yourself then, if you can!" he shouted, his eyes burning in his pale face, his white crown of hair blowing in the wind. She held on to a table of stone some ten feet from the ground, while he climbed above her and beyond, his thin black figure hanging on the smooth surface of the rock. The crying of the hounds was unearthly, coming as it did from the sheet of cloud below, and the sound was increased by the cries and shouting of men, a confusion that filled the air with sound and was the more terrible because it was unseen. The high clouds moved across the sky, and the yellow sun swam into view between them. The cloud below her melted away, and the land that it had covered for so long looked up at the sky, pale and new-born. Mary looked down the sloping hillside; there were little dots of men standing knee-deep in the long grass, while the crying hounds ran in front of them like rats among the fallen rocks.

They followed the track fast, fifty men or more, shouting

and pointing up to the great tables of rock, and as they drew near, the voice of the hounds filled the cracks and the caves. Somebody shouted again, and a man who knelt on the ground scarcely fifty yards from Mary lifted his gun to his shoulder and fired. The shot spat against the granite rock without touching her, and when he rose to his feet she saw that the man was Jem, and that he had not seen her.

The hounds were running in and out among the stones, and one of them jumped up at the rock beneath her. Then Jem fired once more; and, looking beyond her, Mary saw the tall black figure of Francis Davey standing out against the sky, on a wide, flat rock high above her head. He stood for a moment, his hair blowing in the wind; and then he threw his arms wide as a bird throws his wings to fly, and fell—down from his high rock to the wet grass and the little scattered stones.

17

IT was a hard, bright day in early January. The holes in the road, which were generally inches thick in mud or water, were covered with thin ice, and the wheel tracks were white. The air was cold.

Mary walked alone on the moor, and wondered why it was that Kilmar, to the left of her, no longer seemed threatening. The moors were bare still, and the hills were friendless, but the old sense of evil had left them and she could walk upon them without fear. She was at liberty now to go where she chose,. and her thoughts turned to Helford and the green valleys of the south. She had a strange desire in her heart for home and the sight of warm, friendly faces. She remembered with pain every scent and sound that had belonged to her for so long. She belonged to the soil and would return to it again, rooted to the earth as her fathers before her had been. Helford had given her birth, and when she died she would be part of it once more. Only among the woods and streams of her own Helford valley would she know peace and content again.

There was a cart coming towards her from Kilmar, making tracks across the white moor. It was the one moving thing upon the silent plain. She watched it with suspicion, for there were no cottages upon this moor except Trewartha, and Trewartha, she knew, stood empty. Nor had she seen its owner since he had fired past her at Roughtor. "He's an ungrateful devil, like the rest of his family," the magistrate had said. "If I had not helped him, he'd be in prison now, with a long stay before him to break his spirit. I admit he did well. He was the means of finding you, Mary, and that black-coated murderer, but he's never even thanked me for clearing his name in the business, and has taken himself to the world's end, for all I know. There's never been a Merlyn yet that came to any good, and he'll go the same way as the rest of them."

The cart came nearer to the slope of the hill. The horse bent to pull its load, and she saw that it struggled with a strange pile of pots and pans and furniture. Someone was setting out on a journey with his house upon his back. Even then she did not realise the truth, and it was not until the cart was below her and the driver, walking by its side, looked up to her and waved that she recognised Jem.

"Are you better?" he called, from beside the cart. "I heard that you were ill, and had been staying in bed."

"You must have heard wrong," said Mary. "I've been about the house at North Hill. There's never been much the matter with me except a hatred for this neighbourhood."

"There was some talk that you were to settle there, and be a companion to Mrs. Bassat. Well, you'll lead a soft enough life with them, I dare say."

"No. I'm going back home to Helford."

"What will you do there?"

"I shall try to start the farm again, or at least work my way to it, because I haven't the money yet. I've friends there, who will help me at the beginning."

"Where will you live?"

There was a cart coming towards her

"I would be welcome in any cottage in the village. We're good neighbours in the south, you know."

"I've never had neighbours, so I cannot say, but I've had the feeling always that it would be like living in a box, to live in a village. You put your nose over your gate into another man's garden, and if his flowers are better than yours there's an argument; and you know that if you cook a rabbit for your supper he'd have the smell of it in his kitchen. That's no life for anyone! Here's my home, Mary, all the home I've ever had, here in the cart, and I'll take it with me and set it up wherever my fancy takes me. I've been a wanderer since I was a boy; never any ties, nor roots, nor fancies, for any length of time; and I dare say I'll die a wanderer too. It's the only life in the world for me."

"There's no peace, Jem, in wandering, and no quiet. There'll come a time when you'll want your own piece of ground, and your four walls, and your roof, and somewhere to rest your poor, tired bones."

"The whole country belongs to me, Mary, with the sky for a roof and the earth for a bed. You don't understand. You're a woman, and your home is your kingdom. I've never lived like that, and never shall. I'll sleep on the hills one night, and in a city the next. I like to find my fortune here and there and everywhere, with strangers for company and passers-by for friends. Today I meet a man upon the road, and travel with him for an hour or for a year, and tomorrow he is gone again. We speak a different language, you and I."

"Which way will you go?"

"Somewhere east of the river. It doesn't matter to me. I'll never come west again—not until I'm old and grey, and have forgotten many things. I thought of going to the midlands. They're rich up there, and ahead of everyone; there'll be a fortune there for a man who goes to find it. Perhaps I'll have money in my pockets one day, and buy horses for pleasure instead of stealing them."

"It's an ugly black country in the midlands."

"I don't worry about the colour of the soil. Moorland soil

is black, isn't it? And so is the rain when it falls among your pigs down at Helford. What's the difference? "

" You talk just for the sake of argument, Jem: there's no sense in what you say."

" How can I be sensible when you lean against my horse with your hair blowing in the wind? I know that in five or ten minutes' time I shall be over that hill without you. My face will be turned towards the river and you will be walking back to North Hill to drink tea with Mr. Bassat."

" Delay your journey, then, and come to North Hill too."

" Don't be a fool, Mary. Can you see me drinking tea with the magistrate, and dancing his children on my knee? I don't belong to his class, and neither do you."

" I know that. And I am going back to Helford because of it. I want to smell the river again, and walk in my own country."

" Go on, then; turn your back on me and start walking now. You'll come to a road that will take you to Helford."

" You are very hard today, and cruel."

" I am hard with my horses when they are unwilling; but that doesn't mean that I love them any the less."

" You've never loved anything in your life," said Mary.

" I haven't had much use for the word, that's why," he told her. " It's past noon already, and I ought to be on the road. If you were a man I'd ask you to come with me, and you'd jump on to the seat and put your hands in your pockets and ride beside me for as long as it pleased you."

" I'd do that now if you'd take me south."

" Yes, but I'm going north—and you're not a man, you're only a woman, as you'd learn if you came with me. I'm going now. Good-bye."

He took her face in his hands and kissed it, and she saw that he was laughing. " When you're an old woman down in Helford, you'll remember that, and it will have to last you to the end of your days. ' He stole horses,' you'll say to yourself, ' and he didn't care for women; but if I had not been so proud I'd have been with him now.' "

He climbed into the cart and looked down at her, waving his whip. " I'll do fifty miles before tonight," he said, " and sleep like a child at the end of it, in a tent by the side of the road. I'll light a fire, and cook some eggs for my supper. Will you think of me or not? "

But she did not listen; she stood with her face towards the south, hesitating and twisting her hands. Beyond those hills the bare moors turned to green grass, and the green grass to valleys and to streams. The peace and quiet of Helford waited for her beside the running water.

" It's not pride," she told him; " you know it's not pride; there's a sickness in my heart for home and all the things I've lost."

He said nothing, but whistled to the horse. " Wait," said Mary, " wait, and hold him still, and give me your hand."

He laid the whip aside, and reached down to her, and swung her up beside him on the driver's seat.

" What now? " he said. " And where do you want me to take you? You have your back to Helford, do you know that? "

" Yes, I know," she said.

" If you come with me it will be a hard life, and a wild one at times, Mary, with no staying anywhere, and little rest or comfort. You'll get a poor exchange for your farm and little hope of the peace you look for."

" I'll take the risk, Jem."

" Do you love me, Mary? "

" I believe so, Jem."

" Better than Helford? "

" I can't ever answer that."

" Why are you sitting here beside me, then? "

" Because I want to; because I must; because now and for ever more this is where I want to be," said Mary.

He laughed then, and took her hand, and whipped up the horse; and she did not look back over her shoulder again, but set her face northwards towards the river.

QUESTIONS

CHAPTER 1

1. Why had Mary Yellan left her home?
2. Where was she going to live now, and with whom?
3. What seemed strange about her aunt's letter?
4. Why, according to the coach driver, did people avoid Jamaica Inn?
5. How far was the inn from Bodmin?
6. Describe the situation of the inn, and its surroundings.

CHAPTER 2

1. Describe Joss Merlyn.
2. What changes had taken place in Mary's aunt?
3. How did Joss treat his wife?
4. How did Mary show that she was brave?
5. What was Joss's weakness, and what happened when he gave in to it?
6. What did Mary learn about Joss's family?
7. What order did Joss give to Mary as she was going up to bed?

CHAPTER 3

1. Which room in the inn aroused Mary's curiosity?
2. What gave her the chance to explore the country around?
3. Where did she go?
4. What did her uncle tell her on her return?
5. Why, do you think, was Mary losing count of time?
6. Act, or read in parts, the scene between Mary and her aunt.

CHAPTER 4

1. What sort of people came to the inn that night?
2. What did Mary see from her window?
3. How did she explain the scene?
4. Why was she not satisfied with this explanation?
5. What bold thing did she decide to do?

6. Who were the three men who were left outside the inn?
7. What threat did Joss make to the stranger?
8. Who else was at the inn, and where?
9. What did Mary find in the bar?

Chapter 5

1. Why did Mary decide to stay on at Jamaica Inn?
2. How did she explain the rope she had seen in the bar?
3. How did Mary reply to Jem's rudeness?
4. Why was she careful in her answers to his questions?
5. Where did Jem live, and how did he gain his living?
6. What advice did Jem give to Mary?
7. In what ways was Jem like, and in what ways unlike, his elder brother?

Chapter 6

1. What did Mary think might have been the reason for Jem's visit?
2. Why did this thought disappoint her?
3. What gave Mary a chance to tell what she knew?
4. Why did she not take the chance?
5. Why did Mary follow Joss, and with what success?
6. Who rescued her?
7. Describe him.

Chapter 7

1. Why was the vicar alone in the evening?
2. What made Mary tell him everything?
3. What advice did he give her (a) about the smuggling (b) about the murder?
4. What was strange about the vicar's behaviour as they rode over to Jamaica Inn?
5. Why was there no need to explain her absence to Joss?
6. What comfort did the vicar give Mary as he left her?

Chapter 8

1. What change in behaviour came over Mary's aunt and uncle when the latter was drunk for some days?
2. Where did Mary meet Jem?
3. What was the first thing she did on entering his cottage?
4. Whose was the last horse stolen by Jem?
5. What did Jem invite Mary to do?

6. What frightened Joss in his dreams?
7. How many men worked with him, and what was the horrible thing they did?

CHAPTER 9

1. What effect did Mary's new knowledge have on her?
2. What was the other thing that troubled her?
3. To whom did Joss sell the black horse, and for how much?
4. Why did he not wait himself to give the horse to the servant?
5. What Christmas gift did Jem buy for Mary?
6. What did Mary do after waiting in vain for Jem?
7. What had happened to him?
8. How did she get home?
9. What information had been given at the meeting at Launceston?
10. What suggestion did the drunken Joss make to the men?
11. How did he punish Mary for saying she had informed against him?

CHAPTER 10

1. How did Mary get out of the locked carriage?
3. Who was guarding the track?
3. How did Mary escape from him?
4. What was the purpose of the false light?
5. Why did the men leave the wreck half-robbed?
6. Over what did fighting break out, and who won?
7. How were the carriage and the shot men got rid of?

CHAPTER 11

1. How long was Mary in bed?
2. Why was Joss afraid of someone?
3. What was Joss's best chance of saving himself from the law?
4. For what did Harry blame Joss?
5. What suggestion did he make to Joss?
6. What made Joss hit Harry?
7. What was Joss's plan?

CHAPTER 12

1. How did Jem manage to talk to Mary?
2. What did Mary again suspect Jem of being?
3. Why did she ask him to go right away from Jamaica Inn?
4. What did Mary plan to do?
5. Why could she not start before four o'clock?
6. What disappointment awaited her at Altarnun?

Chapter 13

1. What did Mary decide to do?
2. Where had the magistrate gone, and for what purpose?
3. What did Mary fear might happen now?
4. Whom did Mary see at North Hill, that she had seen before?
5. Why did she want to return to the inn?
6. How did she get there?
7. What did she find at the inn?

Chapter 14

1. For what did the magistrate blame Mary, and why?
2. What reason did Mary give for her behaviour?
3. Whom did Mary think had murdered her uncle, and how was this shown to be untrue?
4. What other idea about the murderer came into her mind again?
5. What seemed to support the idea?

Chapter 15

1. What troubled Mary's conscience?
2. What meaning did Mary give to the vicar's strange remarks about the pedlar?
3. How had Mr. Bassat tried to get Jem to bring proof against Joss?
4. Why did Jem at last agree to do so? (See Chapter 12)
5. What had the murderer left behind him?
6. How could the owner be found?

Chapter 16

1. How had Mary interfered with Francis Davey's plans?
2. Why did he kill Joss Merlyn?
3. Why did Mary take the risk of going with him?
4. What made her happy in spite of everything?
5. Why did she not call for help in the village?
6. What helped, and what in the end prevented the escape?
7. Who killed Francis Davey?
8. Find out, if you can, something about albinos in the early ages of man.

Chapter 17

1. What were Mary's plans for the future?
2. What did Jem think she was going to do?
3. What did Jem himself intend to do?
4. What did Mary do in the end?